UNLEASHING THE WRITER WITHIN

UNLEASHING THE WRITER WITHIN

Conquering Self-Doubt

SELLO MOKWENA

Sello Mokwena

CONTENTS

Dedication	vi
One FOREWORD	1
Two INTRODUCTION	3
Three DEALING WITH SELF-DOUBT	7
Four STRATEGIES TO HELP YOU TO OVERCOME SELF-DOUBT	26
Five WHY WRITERS EXPERIENCE SELF-DOUBT	30
Six BEHAVIOURISM	58
Seven THE PYGMALION EFFECT	74
Eight SELF-EFFICACY	94
List of references	108
About The Author	111

This book is dedicated to my late parents, Annah and Stefaan Nyathi

Copyright © 2023 by Sello Mokwena

All rights reserved. No part of this book may be reproduced in any manner whatsoever without written permission except in the case of brief quotations embodied in critical articles and reviews.

Layout and typesetting by Sello Mokwena

Contact Author : sello.mokwena@gmail.com

First Printing, 2023

CHAPTER ONE

FOREWORD

In our societies, there exists a prevailing notion that the art of writing is a skill reserved for a select few, leading to the belief that there is a scarcity of writers. However, we challenge this perception and firmly believe that every individual harbors a unique story within them, waiting to be shared with the world. Countless people effortlessly express their tales, experiences, and emotions on a daily basis through their spoken words. We firmly assert that because you possess the ability to articulate your thoughts and experiences verbally, you equally possess the potential to excel at conveying them through the written word as well.

Sadly, the journey towards becoming a writer is often hindered by the nagging presence of self-doubt. Many aspiring writers find themselves trapped in a cycle of questioning their abilities, doubting the significance of their stories, and fearing the judgments of others. It is this self-doubt that becomes the greatest obstacle, preventing individuals from fully embracing writing as a fulfilling endeavour.

But fear not! The primary objective of this book is to guide you in recognizing the sources of self-doubt and equipping you with practical strategies to overcome its paralyzing grip. We firmly advocate for your right to share your narrative, to give voice to your thoughts and ideas, and to successfully publish your work. Your story matters, and we are here to help you unleash the writer within.

Throughout the pages of this book, we will explore the various facets of self-doubt that commonly plague aspiring writers. We will delve into its origins, dissect its manifestations, and offer empowering tools and techniques to counteract its negative influence. With a combination of guidance, encouragement, and actionable advice, you will develop the confidence needed to embark on your writing journey and create a body of work that resonates with authenticity.

Whether you aspire to pen captivating fiction, thought-provoking essays, or deeply personal memoirs, this book will serve as your compass, leading you past the barriers of self-doubt and towards the realization of your writing dreams. Together, we will navigate the terrain of self-discovery, craft compelling narratives, and celebrate the inherent power of storytelling.

Now is the time to break free from the shackles of self-doubt and embrace your role as a writer. Let us embark on this transformative journey together, as we unlock the potential that lies within you. Get ready to unleash the writer within and share your unique narrative with the world!

CHAPTER TWO

INTRODUCTION

In this book, we are driven by the belief that everyone has the potential to become a good writer. That is, if they receive the necessary coaching and training in scientific writing. Remember that we do not write because we want to; we write because we have to. If you conduct research and do not publish, you are as good as someone who did not even make an attempt. If you have an idea and you never get a way to share it with others - that idea is like a still born baby. Any brilliant thought not put on paper and published it a faint memory that will disappear without trace.

Inexperienced writers often feel overwhelmed by the vast amount of writings produced by other authors, mistakenly believing that these works were completed in a single day. They also hold the misconception that accomplished authors simply woke up one day and became skilled writers. However, this couldn't be further from the truth. Everyone has to start somewhere. The primary goal of this book is to instill confidence in you, guiding you step by step along the way. Writing is a gradual process, akin to constructing a magnificent building. You should understand that any magnificent building you admire was built brick by brick, line by line. The sheer magnitude of the task can be daunting. Remember, writing is accomplished one day at a time. As the saying goes, Rome wasn't built in a day!

Many new writers and researchers suffer from self-doubt when they are supposed to publish their work for the world to see what they have achieved throughout their research process. Self-doubt often accompanies all individuals who want to share their inner selves with the world. Self-doubt whispers in a gentle tone that resonates solely within you. It insidiously declares your inadequacy, questions your intelligence, undermines your talent, and suggests that you are unworthy of being heard.

At the heart of self-doubt is a fear or belief that you are not good enough. That's not true — you are good enough just as you are now. Do not be afraid to share your unique stories with the world through your writing.

What if great writers, such as William Shakespeare, Matsepe, Chinua Achebe, had let the fear of not being good enough stop them from writing? I wonder how many other potentially great writers did not become well known because self-doubt held them back.

Not everything you write will be excellent. If you read the works of famous and prolific writers, you will find that the same is true for them. After all, they are (or were) human beings, just like you and me. On the other hand, if you are careful and diligent, most of your work will be good enough to delight and inspire your audience. Ultimately, that's all you need.

Self-doubt is normal and maybe even necessary. Every writer has moments of self-doubt, although when it happens, you definitely feel as though you are the only one with the self-doubt problem. Self-doubt is something every writer will face in one way or another. What you need to know is that there are strategies you will learn in this book to overcome negative feelings. You need to know that the messages you receive from self-doubt are devoid of any truth.

Sara Cannon in her blog post entitled "How to overcome self-doubt as A Writer", contends that doubt is at its worst when you first try to decide what to write about, what topic or idea to follow. You may ask yourself whether what you intend to write is going to be good or unique enough. The insecurity produced by lack of self-belief may trigger some reservations in your mind.

Doubt may also creep in at the heart of the writing process when things start to get daunting. You may start feeling as if this is the worst book or article you have ever written and that it will never come together. Doubt may raise its ugly head during the thick of edits when you are trying to make your ideas come together in a meaningful way and it is not coming out as well as you planned or envisaged. At this stage, you may think that doubt will leave you alone, but when you sent the manuscript for an initial review to a second set of eyes before it sent to the editor or to a journal or the publisher, doubt comes back more forcefully. Once you hit the send button the work is no longer in your hands and you have to wait for feedback.

Self-doubt wreaks havoc when you are not careful and pay more than necessary attention to the successes of other people. You may find that you compare yourself too much with those you think do not suffer from self-doubt. You may generate emotions of worry and wrongly believe that you will never live up to the perceived high unrealistic standard. These comparisons may leave you feeling low and demotivated.

Receiving a negative review or comment can be devastating if you fail to differentiate between criticism of your manuscript and criticism of yourself as an author. Recall that the objective of the review or comments is to improve the work and not to improve your self-worth. The reviewers are not criticising you!! but the work!! And the good thing is that the work can and must be improved. Sometimes we get more positive reviews than negative ones, but our hearts are completely broken by one negative review. Sometimes, this is how the mind functions. When you look at a white paper, you notice one small black dot and ignore the rest of the white paper.

In the next sections, we are going to look at strategies and tactics of dealing with self-doubt. We will also look at theories of behaviour that my help to explain why we react the way we do to different situations. These theories will help you to understand your own behaviour and the behaviour of those around you. You will be able to make a soberer judgment about yourself. You may even develop sympathy for those around you as you will have some clue about the motivations behind their actions and reactions. People are always trying their best with the resources at their disposal. Sometimes you may think people go out of their way to be nasty, whereas they are actually expressing their own insecurities. If you understand their background, it may aid you to absorb their criticism much better; unlike if you do not have a basic understanding of human behaviour.

We will expand on general principles which you may find helpful in dealing with discouragement and despondency. I hope after going through this book you come out as a strong-minded person with the determination of turning every obstacle into a stepping stone and every lemon into lemonade.

"Writing is finally about one thing: going into a room alone and doing it. I put words on paper that have never been there quite that way before. And although you are physically by yourself, the haunting Demon never leaves you, that Demon being the knowledge of your own terrible limitations, your hopeless inadequacy, the impossibility of ever getting it right. No matter how diamond-bright your ideas dance in your brain, on paper they are earthbound."
William Goldman, Adventures in the Screen Trade

Happy reading!!

CHAPTER THREE

DEALING WITH SELF-DOUBT

'Our doubts are traitors, and make us lose the good we might win, by fearing to attempt.' - William Shakespeare, Measure for Measure

'If you hear a voice within you saying that you cannot write, then by all means write and that voice will be silenced.' Vincent Willem van Gogh

In this chapter, we deal with some tips that you can use to deal with self-doubt as a writer. Take these tips into heart and let them be your companions on your writing journey. As authors we are people who are doing good to society today and to posterity in general. The ideas you put on paper are bound in one way or another to help somebody you may never even
meet. This is one reason among many that you need to keep in mind as you put self-doubt under control - for this is the enemy we may never be able to defeat completely.

Keep Going.

Sometimes, the only way out of a situation is through that situation. Winners never quit, and quitters never win. Self-doubt can be overwhelming, and you may get the impression that the only logical action is to give up. Don't quit, keep going. Because if you do not give up, you are guaranteed to be victorious.

You owe it to yourself to finish what you have started. As a writer, you cannot be ruled by excitement and moods, where you write a few paragraphs and when you start feeling stuck, you get overwhelmed by self-doubt. You think starting a new manuscript will make you feel better and then you get stuck again. If you allow yourself to go through this merry-go-round, the same feeling of being stuck will haunt you, unless you decide to do something else. The key solution lies in mustering the courage, regardless of the challenges involved, and allowing your determination to propel you towards completing the manuscript. Keep going! You must believe that you will be able to complete your writing project successfully.

Setbacks can easily cause you to doubt yourself and throw you off course. If you send an article to a journal or a manuscript to a publisher and you get a response telling you that it has been rejected, accept the disappointment, then dust yourself off and try again. Failure to acknowledge your circumstances will result in distress and de-motivation. As the saying goes, transform your obstacles into opportunities or convert adversity into advantage. Take a moment to collect your thoughts and objectively assess the feedback provided by reviewers. Often, this process can provide valuable insights on how to revise your paper or manuscript, enabling you to submit it to a different journal or publisher. Understand this setback as a way to learn and move forward. Read the reasons for the rejection carefully, so that you can soberly determine your next course of action.

Most journals and book publishers discourage destructive criticism from reviewers and urge them to point out how the author can improve their work. They encourage the reviewers to be specific in their comments. Some reviewers have a tendency to comment only on mistakes in a paper or manuscript. They are now encouraged to also point out the good aspects of the paper. The review process is now a developmental rather than a punitive process. The review should give suggestions on how the article can be improved. If they reject the paper, they should furnish detailed reasons for the rejection.

Constructive criticism is highly specific and includes suggestions for improvement. It does not attack you as a person but focuses on a particular point or issue. The person who delivers it intends to help you grow and improve, rather than put you down. So, if the criticism was not constructive, just let it go. Don't let it bother you. It is just one person's opinion, after all. See how and what you can learn from the feedback.

Become a good student

There is a saying that: "when the learner is ready the teacher will appear". Sometimes authors experience self-doubt because of this high standard that we have in our minds about how we want to be as writers. Only to find that during the writing process our initial view of ourselves as the brilliant writer we thought we were going to be is tested to the limit. Reality and perception are sometimes not bedfellows. We must always do our best and not worry when we are not the best. As we craft our writing, we are bound to fall short. We should never be afraid to miss the mark. We must become lifelong learners who are actively learning. Become an avid reader of books on how to be a better writer. Get as many writing tools as possible on how to write better. And how to write a better introduction, abstract, and conclusion. Listen to the comments of your supervisor or mentor. Some mistakes by new writers include long sentences, no links to paragraphs, and erroneous punctuation. Long sentences lead to loss of intended meaning. Make use of short sentences to preserve the meaning. Ideally, each sentence should contain one clear idea. If there are too many ideas in one sentence, it may confuse the reader. Once the reader gets confused, you have lost them. Remember that you are writing for your readers and not for yourself. Your reviews are the first main target audience are writing for, because they are the gatekeepers for your readers. If you cannot convince your reviews, your work may not see the light of day. Make your writing interesting and captivating.

There should be clear links between the paragraphs. Your paragraphs should be seamlessly connected. Often we forget that writing is like storytelling. In everyday conversations we link our thoughts, we do not move from one thought to another disconnected idea. Our ideas flow naturally and it allows the listener to understand what we are talking about. But often when it comes to writing, we tend to throw words around in a meaningless manner. You find that the next paragraph has nothing to do with the previous one.

Punctuation is another area that we need to learn. Putting a comma in the wrong place can completely alter your sentence. Putting a full stop before the sentence is complete can turn off your reader. Fortunately, we have grammar and spelling checkers built into most word processing programs. Sometimes all you need to do is to turn these features on in your program. There are also free-to-use writing tools on the Web. Use them to improve your writing.

Another way to improve your writing is to be a good observant reader. Check how other authors use short sentences. Look at how they use punctuation to keep the meaning of their sentences. Keep an eye out for the manner in which they link their paragraphs.

Learn how to edit your manuscript using the available writing tools. This will enable you to improve your writing. The Internet is full of resources that can help you to be improve your writing. There are blogs and even videos. You are not the first person to try your hand at writing. There are many others who have come before you. On social networks, people are freely sharing their experiences, which may sometimes be helpful. You are not alone; you are part of a worldwide community. Give yourself the best possible chance to be your very best. Don't compete to be better than other people. Instead become your own competition. Become a better you every day.

Self-doubt is sometimes triggered by fear that causes you to think that maybe you are not going to be the best writer. You need to be comforted by the knowledge that everyone feels this way sometimes. Nobody became a good writer before they started writing. To get through these moments, it may be helpful to remind yourself that it is fine not to be the best all the time. Do not delay writing because you are afraid that you will make mistakes. Perfectionism is sometimes the enemy of progress.

Mistakes can be fixed later.

You cannot edit a blank page. This is so simple and basic, but most of us are reluctant to put the pen on paper due to self-doubt. Even a poorly written piece of work, if it is written in black and white, offers you a lot to labour with. Do not worry if it is not good enough the first time. One way to win against your own self-doubts is to continue putting words on the page, taking baby steps. Rome was not built in one day, but it was built one day at a time.

Despite its apparent simplicity the idea of just Keeping on writing is the most effective approach to conquering self-doubt. Try to stop thinking about what you're writing. Just let your fingers flow over the keyboard. Don't worry if it sounds like nonsense. Concentrate on getting the first draft down as quickly as possible without rereading what you've written. Don't judge, criticise or compare yourself. Write especially when you don't feel like it.

Self-doubt can stop you from writing in subtle ways. You may think, "I have nothing to write about today" or "No one will want to read my writing." Neither of these statements are true. You never know when one of your pieces will resonate with a lot of people and become popular. But even if a piece isn't popular, it's still successful if it helps a few people.

So do not let negative thoughts hold you back. Keep your daily writing habits as much as possible. Don't beat yourself up if you miss a day, but also don't make excuses for yourself if you miss several days due to self-defeating thoughts. Don't be discouraged by bad days.

We all have bad days. Days when we can't string a coherent sentence together. Days when nothing we write seems to make logical sense. Days when, no matter how hard we try, we don't seem to achieve anything.

Don't let those days discourage you or, worse still, stop you from writing. Just accept that you will have some days like that, as all writers do, and believe that tomorrow will be better. Tomorrow is usually a better day, especially if you begin with a positive attitude and a positive affirmation, such as: 'I am an excellent writer," or "I write easily and effortlessly". As a general rule it is better to look forward rather than backward. The grammatical mistakes and wrong spelling are going to be fixed during the editing process. During the process of editing, your writing is going to be subjected to panel beating. This is the time to fix and improve your writing. Fortunately, in the technology era, we have the tools to help you with this process. But those tools can only help you when you have started the writing process. If you use Microsoft Word, there is a thesaurus you can use to select appropriate words. If you go on reviews ribbon you find the thesaurus. If you select a word you want to improve the thesaurus gives you a list of alternative words. Select the one most appropriate for the point you are trying to make. With these tools you suddenly expand your vocabulary. For every writing aspect there are tools to speed up your work. We will look into writing tools in details in the last chapter of this book.

Clearly your manuscript will have to be correct in every respect for publication. Doubts may resurface just when you are supposed to send the work away. When you have corrected all you needed to correct it is time to send the work away irrespective of your doubts at this stage. Keep writing although you feel scared and you may be struggling to get words on the paper because you think they are not good enough.

What sometimes helps during the writing process, when you're experiencing a self-doubt-filled day, it's a good idea to look at and appreciate some of your published work, that is if you have already published your work. If you have not yet published your work but you have completed your research work you may read that work to encourage yourself that you have written a good piece of work. This may help you to move past self-doubt by giving you a quick confidence boost.

Read your favourite parts

It is important to have people who can read your work before you sent it to the publishers. These people are sometimes called critique partners. When you are writing, you may be too subjective to judge the quality of your work. Even if you have a supervisor in the process of academic writing your supervisor is also too close to the work and may miss somethings. This is why when you think that you have finished your writing, it becomes important to have this person or persons who can read your work and give you genuine feedback with no consideration for your feelings. Keep in mind that the feedback is not aimed at your ego but at improving the work. Do not take feedback personally. When you receive negative feedback, do not think of running away or hiding. Most probably, the feedback will not be a blanket criticism of your work. Open the manuscript and read it carefully and then look at the feedback, you will see that there are some good things about your work. If you have passed any research subject, go back and read that report or thesis and remind yourself that you have published something successfully before. Picking any part of your previous writing that you wrote strengthens your hand and mind, that you are capable of doing a good job. There are certain behaviours that may trigger self-doubt and it important that you are able to identify them.

Self-Doubt Triggering Behaviours

So far we have covered the things you can do to overcome self-doubt. In this section we deal with what not, to do. You need to guard against certain behaviours that do not help you pertaining to your self-confidence. The first devastating self-sabotaging behaviour is with comparing yourself to other writers. This has proven to be the quickest way to worsen your self-doubt. If you read reviews of your work and concentrate on the negative parts, it is not going to help you at all. If you reduce the totality of your writing to the negative parts of your review, this will feed into reducing your self-confidence. Avoid, as far as humanly possible, spending time with people who incessantly, negatively criticise you or disparage your capabilities. Some friends or critique partners who do not believe in your dreams as a writer must be avoided. Do not wallow in self-pity by staring at a blank page, and believe that you have not accomplished much even if you wrote one paragraph, that day. That is enough for one day.

If you are not aware of the self-doubt-generating behaviours, you cannot stop them. As they say knowing what the problem is, is half the solution. If you can become aware of these behaviours, you are halfway to stopping them. The sooner, the better. It is vital to cultivate mindfulness and self-awareness.

Mindfulness entails directing one's attention and intention towards the present moment. It involves the deliberate cultivation of conscious awareness. Engaging in mindfulness requires adopting an open, receptive, and non-judgmental attitude, allowing things to be observed and accepted as they are without the urge to alter them. By practicing mindfulness, one can experience a state of relaxation and non-judgmental awareness concerning the body and mind. In this state, the emphasis is not on attaining specific outcomes, regardless of how desirable they may seem.

Mindfulness techniques have a meditative component. Formal mindfulness meditation techniques include mindfulness or awareness of your body and your movements. They also incorporate being aware and in the present moment as much as possible, even during such seemingly mundane tasks as brushing one's teeth.

The primary purpose of self-awareness is to alleviate psychological distress and facilitate personal growth. It serves as a pathway to self-development, enabling individuals to cultivate psychological well-being. Self-awareness in addition to mental health substantially impacts day-to-day functioning of an individual. It promotes and improves performance. With reflection and mindfulness individuals get the courage to persist with tasks despite performance-related stress.

If you find yourself in any group of writers for example, social media groups, where most of them are forever bragging about their accomplishments. This is likely to affect how you feel about yourself and your writing journey. If these groups are not helping you, you need to question your membership of the groups. Even though you may learn some good and helpful tips and tricks along the way from these groups, and yet if they trigger self-doubt which keeps you from writing, the question is, are they worth your time? You should check yourself if you are not one of these people who have the habit of sending negative messages to themselves about how bad they are all the time. If you tell yourself that you will not finish what you have started and that you will never be published, know that these are self-defeating thoughts. Only you have the power to stop that kind of thinking.

Bad behaviour patterns and habits are easy to pick up but too difficult to break down. Dealing with these behaviour patterns and habits is imperative to keep your mental health. Your career as a writer will also benefit. Recognising the destructive behaviours is a new skill you have to learn, so that every time these behaviours rear their ugly head you can notice them and deal with them accordingly. Positive self-talk is important to help you to develop a positive frame of mind. Your happiness is your choice. Happiness is a remedy for self-doubt.

In the following paragraphs, we share some insights about some of the behaviours that you should avoid in dealing with self-doubt.

"I seek strength, not to be greater than other, but to fight my greatest enemy, the doubts within myself"
P.C. Cast

Avoid comparison with more experienced authors

When you are new to writing, just like a child you will have to start by crawling and when you have mastered walking you can run. You will be blundering if you start comparing yourself to writers who have been in the game for a long time. Remember that they started where you are now and not where they are today. Every writer is running their own race. Good advice is to run your own race without looking left or right. It is obvious that if you don't look ahead when you run, you may easily stumble. Remember you are not competing with anybody. As a writer, your destiny is exclusively yours. Your success is fully in your hands. It all depends on how far you want to go. There will be obstacles, but with perseverance and the will to succeed you are on the right track.

Even after learning all skills we have suggested in this book self-doubt will not be eliminated completely. If it crawls in, you may have to prioritise your work and start with the first task on the list. Compare yourself to where you started, and you will see the progress you are making. You may not be where you want to be but you are not where you started. The images and messages of people you see on social media may not always be a true reflection. Remember that most of the times the postings that we see on social media sites are carefully selected. In the pictures people chose to pose in such a way that the photos are taken from the best angles possible. And then the photos are filtered. The image you perceive does not always accurately reflect a person's true essence. This concept also applies to observing other authors as they navigate their paths toward publishing books or articles. Frequently, individuals tend to share their triumphs with others, showcasing their achievements. Seldom do people share their weaknesses and challenges.

Often people do not share their struggles. The reality is that the struggle is the part of life for everyone. The ups and downs of life are perfectly normal. It is through these ups and downs that we are able to grow and become better.

There is no standard path to success. Everyone succeeds differently. That is why what produces attainment for one person might not work for you. There is not a one-size-fits-all success recipe. If you want to avoid writer self-doubt, do not compare yourself to others. You are on the right path, if you keep on doing the right things you are doing now, you will ultimately reach your destination. Keep working and believing Be patient with yourself. Success is the result of investing time and consistent effort. There is no overnight success.

"Never let fear hold you captive.
Never let self-doubt hold you captive.
Never let frustration hold you captive."
  Roy T. Bennett, The Light in the Heart,

Ask for help

For those who are new to writing, accept that you are a novice to the writing process. There is no shame in asking for help when you are stuck. Being ashamed to ask for help means that you will be stuck longer than necessary. You must accept that you are new to writing. Asking for help should not embarrass you. Even if you are an old hand, asking for help does not go out of fashion.

Reach out to more experienced authors and you be surprised how people are willing to help you if you ask. They are mentors who are readily available with great advice. They will assist you on how to proceed with your manuscript. There are plenty of online writing communities where people share their writing experiences. Here you can gain writing wisdom from many authors. With modern technology, your advice is not confined to your immediate physical environment. You can find people online who are eager to lend a helping hand.

Guard against the inner critic

Self-doubt is rooted in deeply ingrained negative beliefs that have been shaped over time by various influences such as teachers, parents, relatives, friends, and even strangers. These beliefs can leave us feeling stagnant and lacking inspiration. Examples of such negative beliefs include doubting the quality of your work, thinking it is not good enough to be published by prestigious publications or specific journals. Many writers unknowingly become victims of their own harsh "inner critic", failing to recognize the subjective nature of that critical voice. This voice may come from your childhood experiences rather than being a voice of reason as we often assume. If you have experienced a lack of self-confidence and self-love in your early years it makes you more susceptible to paralyzing self-doubt. Self-doubt emerges as a protective mechanism, shielding us from potential pain. By avoiding to write altogether, one can evade the possibility of facing criticism or rejection.

You are going to develop a new self-talk to motivate yourself to be the best version of yourself. To succeed as a writer, avoid certain words. You cannot tell yourself that you are not good enough. These types of words should be eliminated from your vocabulary. Although developing this new mind set maybe challenging. These new skills are necessary to reach your desired goal of being a published writer.

Positive thinking is a precursor to positive action. A positive life is a result of positive actions. In order to become a good author, you have to find ways of shutting down the inner critical voice. That "inner critic" is a persistent nuisance! Many of us struggle with this inner critic that causes us to stop and put breaks in our path to success. We need to be smarter than the inner critic and work smarter in order to overcome this challenge. That inner critical voice will persist in attempting to create doubts in your mind. It is up to you to let it win. Once the critical voice in your head takes the upper hand, it is going to be difficult for you to find your way out. You cannot prevent a bird from flying over your head, but it is up to you prevent it from buiding a nest on your head - that is your choice! When you realise that the critical voice is on the prowl, you can use the phrases below to diffuse that negative inner voice:

"Stop!"
"I'm better than this!"

"You won't bring me down!"
"No! I have this!"
'I can do this.'
'I am smart / talented / skilled.'
'I'm not perfect, but I'm doing the best I can.'
"What if I fall? Oh, no!!, what if I fly?"

Trepidation and misgiving take over when you pay too much attention on the prospect of falling. When your focus is on the chance of flying, then you have set yourself free. This is freedom from self-imposed limitations, which will banish fear, doubt, and insecurity. This will enable you to step into a new world where you will experience, adventure, passion and possibility. Starve the inner critical voice by beginning to reject those negative doubts as not belonging to you. Actions emanate from thoughts. You create your life from actions, so make sure to preserve positive thoughts as far as it is humanly possible. Bad days come for everyone.

Don't be discouraged by bad Days

If you have not experienced rejection as a writer, you have not started writing. Novelists and scientists spend their precious time developing their writing. The authors write and have to check for plagiarism by editing and re-editing their work. In this process they worry about the smallest word. Notwithstanding this hard work, it does not mean the publishers will automatically accept the manuscript. Famous books like the Harry Porter series were rejected by several publishers, only to become best sellers later. We all have bad days. Days when we can't string a coherent sentence together. Days when nothing we write seems to make logical sense. Days when, no matter how hard we try, we don't seem to be achieve anything.

Don't let those days discourage you or, worse still, stop you from writing. Just accept that you will have some days like that, as all writers do, and believe that tomorrow will be better. Tomorrow is usually a better day, especially if you begin with a positive attitude and a positive affirmation, such as: 'I am an excellent writer," or "I write easily and effortlessly."

Know what Makes You Feel Great

Look for positive reinforcement that will help you create a distance between you and self-doubt. This will enable you to get back on the road and get you excited to write and enjoy it. The following are some of the activities that can be helpful.

- Create a vision board based on what you like about the writing process. The occasion when you get discouraged, visit the vision board and remind yourself why you like writing with all your heart.
- Create a set of good phrases. Read them when you receive a bad review. You can also read them when you or experience a particularly tough day in your writing journey. In some of the phrases you can tell yourself that you are a great writer. It is important that you believe in what you have written. What you believe often comes to pass. If you are a religious person you can find writings in your holy book that can be helpful when you are dealing with a bad day, a bad person or even a tough day at the office.
- Write your experience in a notebook. Put all things that have bothered you on paper. Write also about your pleasant experiences. Never forget the reason you have started writing. Keep your goals in mind. The journaling session should not focus on your doubts only.
- By this time, you know the people who believe in you and those who have no confidence in your abilities. This is the time to talk to those who believe in you as a writer.

- If you have fans or people who have read your work in the past, you can read some of their positive messages. Whenever you receive positive messages, make sure to save them in a notebook or file on your computer so you can go back to them when you are in doubt.
- Develop an active life style. Do a thing which will lift you up like watching a favourite movie. You may join the running or cycling club in your vicinity. You may even join an amateur club of your favourite sport.
- Create a curated collection of songs to form a musical playlist. Music possesses a remarkable ability to provide solace and comfort. I recommend selecting a few cherished songs that you can listen to whenever needed. Your playlist should serve as a source of inspiration, motivation, and serve as a reminder of why you exert significant effort in pursuing your goals.

When doubts and negative emotions begin to overpower you, adhere to the aforementioned routines. Consider singing passionately and even dancing around the room if it won't inconvenience others. Allow yourself to tap into the reservoir of motivation and confidence that may have been buried within. Rekindle that inner fire and embrace a renewed sense of determination.

If you are starting as a new writer, you can be sure that self-doubt regarding your writing abilities and the degree to which you can succeed as a writer will attack you. You must expect this kind of feeling. To succeed as a writer, these fears and concerns have to be overcome. In this next section, we would like to give you the tools to use to overcome these fears. Writers Republic offers seven ideas to overcome the fear of writing, which are discussed below.

Take it one step at a time.

If you want to get to the upstairs room of a high-rise building, you will either use the lift or the stairs. You do not jump to the room of an upstairs building. Beside not comparing yourself to fellow writers as we have already discussed, the other precaution you should be aware of is to be careful not to be haste when you are writing or editing your work. Go about your writing in a systematic manner and enjoy the journey without worrying about the destination. There is no need to pressurise yourself. Pressure will result in shoddy work. Slow and surely, for they stumble that run fast. Everyone need to develop a writing style. Expose yourself to many writing styles as possible, because that may help you to develop your own writing style This will put you several steps ahead. It is better to take time to sharpen your axe instead of using a blunt one. A blunt axe, requires more time and energy.

Right frame of mind

Writing is mentally taxing, and requires you to be in a good mental space. Establish what motivates you. These motivations will allow you to stay the writing course. Rest is important and rejuvenates you, so give yourself enough time to rest and recharge. If you are well rested, your mind will be at its best and will enable you to completely focus on the writing process. Try to resolve whatever anxieties you may have. If you are feeling scared or unmotivated, self-help and motivational books may help. I you belong to a particular religion your holy book may have writings that may help you. Look for any exercise that will keep you motivated, to ensure you are in the right frame of mind and prepared for the writing process.

Encircle yourself with helpful people.

"Criticism is just someone else's opinion. Even people who are experts in their fields are sometimes wrong. It is up to you to choose whether to believe some of it, none of it, or all of it. What you think is what counts."
—— Rodolfo Costa, *Advice My Parents Gave Me: and Other Lessons I Learned from My Mistakes*

As a general rule of thumb for any area of your life, make sure that you always surround yourself with positive people. Positive people who believe in you will help you easily defeat doubting yourself as a writer, whereas negative people will increase self-doubt.

Positive people will cause the writing process to be enriching and enable you to enjoy the writing journey. Encircling yourself with helpful people is a great support system. That will make the writing process trouble-free and enjoyable. Avoid negative people because they focus on the impossible and are able to find a fault even in the best situation possible, they will drain your energy. And as we have already seen, writing requires a lot of energy.

Having someone to turn to for inspiration makes the life journey rewarding and this may spill over into writing motivation. These are people who will be there, rain or shine, dark or blue. They are your number one fans. They form your support system in good times and in bad times.

When doubts start attacking you, these are the kind of person you want to have in your corner. They will remind you of your greatness at the time when your self-belief fades and self-doubt knocks at your door. This positive persons or people are the ones who always believes in you and is willing to do everything in their power to see you succeed. Do you have someone to lift you up? Who believes in you? Who helps you to think great of yourself? Who lifts you up in writing? You can see that you need someone to believe in you, so also believe in someone whom you can lift up when they need to be encouraged.

Be courageous

The writing process is going to test your character to the limit. Your character will be tested in a way you never thought possible, right through the writing process. Courage is going to be required in great quantities. On the surface it looks like to be a writer is an easy job. Because writing is not a child's play, you need courage to succeed. You will need to be willing to take chances. Successful people know how to brush off criticisms and doubts when things don't go their way. So you will need nerves of steel to succeed. Be kind and patient to yourself on those days when doubt is too strong, because doubt can never be completely annihilated, sometimes it takes the center stage. Develop a comeback strategy from the tips we have shared so far.

As a writer you need a tough skin. Critics are some fault-finders who will point out to you all your shortcomings during your moments of weakness. Critics are everywhere, so you should be prepared for them or they can trip you unawares. Maintain an openness to learning from feedback, even when it comes from individuals who may not necessarily have your best interests at heart. Recognize that valuable insights can still be gleaned from their perspectives, regardless of their intentions. Don't take your writing work personally. Listen to every critic with an open mind and see if you can find something helpful from their negative criticism. In order to respond to self-doubt in a healthy way as a writer, you start with self-respect. The next step is to think of yourself in a positive way. Handle yourself with care. Be conscious of the way you treat yourself. Develop confidence and love yourself. Part of developing great self-belief is to prepare very well.

"Success is where preparation and opportunity meet." Bobby Unser

"Proper preparation prevents poor performance." Stephen Keague

"There are no secrets to success. It is the result of preparation, hard work, and learning from failure." Colin Powell

Do your research thoroughly.

Please don't commit avoidable mistakes like not having your facts right or grammatical errors which can be picked up by a speller checker. Use a good document management system. Keep all versions of your work by creating folders for everything. Sometimes we become our own enemies by not doing our work with diligence. If your work is done well in a careful manner you will minimize the unnecessary criticism of your work. You cannot do the best with your writing without research. Research as thoroughly as possible. The references should be double-checked for correctness and currency. All in-text references should be on the reference list and vice versa. Should anyone call your facts into question you can defend yourself from your organised list of your sources.

Another thing that can protect you against self-doubt is to believe that you are good, smart, talented and worthy enough to be heard. This will put down the voice of doubt.

It's a bonus to hear positive feedback from other people, but more importantly, you must give yourself the same positive feedback you expect from others. Hearing and believing the positive feedback is essential.

The purpose of this book is to enable you to excel in your writing and put your worries at ease. There is no need to reinvent the wheel. Learn form what others who came before have done.

If you need to rest, take a break from your writing work to recuperate. If you find yourself not making progress leave the writing work for a while and focus on something else for a short time in order to recover and then you can go back to your work.

You need to be careful not to be caught in the "busy-ness" trap. This is when you just want to appear to be busy but there are not results to show for your business. They say burnout never comes from hard work, but from working hard without results to show. Even as you put in the time and spent sleepless nights to meet your deadlines also develop a systems of networks around yourself. That is, you need to work smarter even as you work hard. Create great rapport with your publishers and all other stakeholders to you journey to publishing your work

"Don't let others tell you what you can't do. Don't let the limitations of others limit your vision. If you can remove your self-doubt and believe in yourself, you can achieve what you never thought possible." - Roy T. Bennett, The Light in the Heart

CHAPTER FOUR

STRATEGIES TO HELP YOU TO OVERCOME SELF-DOUBT

"Believe in yourself, your abilities and your own potential. Never let self-doubt hold you captive. You are worthy of all that you dream of and hope for.'
—— Roy Bennett

In this section we share strategies to help you overcome self-doubt so that you can do more writing and less self-sabotaging.

Be aware of your self-doubt.

When confronting your "inner critic", it will help you if you know your strengths and weaknesses. Doubts is like a thief that comes in when you are not ready. Doubt will not knock on your door. Doubt comes in when you least expect it and takes you by surprise! If you know your strengths and weaknesses, it will assist you to know when the critical voice is trying to steer you off course. By now you know and hopefully you have come to accept that self-doubt is part and parcel of the experience of every writer. This acknowledgment will help you to fight the negative feelings brought about by doubt. Because you know that doubt is part of the package, when it hits you, you will not quit. If you are not an expert on a particular topic, read some more to expand your knowledge. Your voice deserves to be heard. You never know who will benefit from your writing as much as the many authors whose work you have read do not know how their work has impacted you.

Awareness of your talents will enable you to put them to good use. Appreciate your strengths and talents. Believe that you are talents and strength are not less than those of the best authors. Because you are reading this book and you have read this far means you have that desire to improve yourself and your situation. You are one of a kind, and you need to see yourself in the same light.

To have come up to so far in this book means that you want to improve yourself. The actions that you are taking every day are bringing you closer to achieving your goals and confronting self-doubt head-on.

We all have weaknesses. It's a strength to accept your weaknesses. Weaknesses are a sign that you are human. There is no perfect human being. We all have something we need to work on. It takes time to improve and become better. Hard work, determination, patience, and our skill-set are a means to overcome our weaknesses. Working on your weaknesses is worth your energy and time.

Weaknesses are not supposed to be a judgement on your character or proof that you are not good enough. It is an indication that you may have to put more effort in that particular area. Doubts like to cling to your weaknesses, but don't let them! If you know something is going to happen then you are able to prepare for it. When a predictable event takes place you are not surprised. Setbacks are part of life.

Setbacks will happen.

When you experience a setback, it may feel as if this writing stuff is not for you. I want to assure you that it doesn't mean you are suddenly not meant to be an author. Setbacks may mean you need to identify the problems, so you can properly address them. Other authors have been where you are today in their writing journey - and are willing help you to address your situation. There is always someone who has experienced, what you are going through now, and may be willing to help you. There are so many incredible authors who have walked this path and know the journey you are traveling. They are willing to help and guide you along the way.

Find a community of authors online. There are many if you google them. These are like-minded people who have been through this process before. Some are like you, grappling with the same kind of problems your are dealing with. These may be even more helpful to you as they are experiencing problems at the same level as yourself. These may have some fresh ideas and are eager to help and lend support. There are writer's conferences which you can attend. Here you will meet other writers who understand your journey and can support you along the way.

Past failures can lead to writers' self-doubt. The doubts which are fed by the previous fears may trap us in fear. We all have failed in the past. You also you have failed in the past. We cannot allow ourselves to wallow in the past but learn from that experience and move on. This is an opportunity for growth and gratitude rather than allowing self-doubt to win. Sometimes people in your life may contribute to your setback.

Some people close to you may not understand your reasons or mindset and as such they may start to question why you're doing what you're doing. Some may even try to bring you down and sow the seed of doubt and amplify that voice that is telling you, that you cannot accomplish your goal which is important to you. The good news is that you can prevent them from discouraging you.

Don't seek approval from these kinds of people, especially when you're working on something you hold so dear to your heart. This questioning can cause doubt to flood in again. You must be on the lookout for this type of situation.

These setbacks make the reward at the end even more grand! I promise it will be worth it when you hold your published book or article in your two hands.

Celebrate your victories

Being a published author is a major achievement. It becomes extra special if your book or article is in demand. By the way, it is not everyone who accomplishes this. When your work is published it will be a great time of celebration. Celebrate having recognised those inevitable moments of self-doubt and faced them head-on and not allowed them to stop you from being called a published author. Remember the price that lay ahead when you are facing self-doubt. It is strange how these simple concepts are sometimes the most challenging to achieve. Know what you stand for and be strong in your voice. Belief in yourself and your abilities, even when doubt tries to strike.

Begin facing self-doubt as a writer today so you can reach the success and happiness you desire in your personal life and your career.

Some authors at the beginning of the writing journey anticipate that exhaustion or writers' self-doubt would creep in some days. They prepare for the road ahead by drafting an inspirational poster. Whenever they needed motivation, they read the poster which quickly remind them that their mission is too important to allow doubts to take over. You can make your own poster by writing quotes that are meaningful to you and hang them somewhere in your home as a reminder to face self-doubt head on. There are examples of an inspirational posters on the Internet. Please check them and learn how you can write yours.

By conquering your self-doubt and learning how to stop it in its tracks when it creeps up, you will have more time to write and less time sulking.

CHAPTER FIVE

WHY WRITERS EXPERIENCE SELF-DOUBT

I am always in self-doubt... every moment of my filmmaking. I am supremely confident when the story is being written and everything is in our head. But the moment we get into the filmmaking, I start doubting myself - from the camera angle to the re-recording to getting the actors to do their shots. - S. S. Rajamouli

Dana Shavin conducted research about why writers experience self-doubt . In her research, she addressed the following questions:

- What drives self-doubt?
- Do society and culture play a role?
- Is self-doubt a by-product of self-revelation?
- Is the crowded marketplace to blame?

She formulated the questions with the aim of getting people to think about why writers are prone to such harsh, debilitating self-talk? What drives this self-doubt? Do society and culture play a role? Is the crowded marketplace to blame? 'When can I call myself a writer?" as if there were some invisible threshold over which we must spin in order to earn the coveted title? Does self-doubt ever decrease? Is the publication a cure for self-doubt?

Dana in conducting her research submitted a questionnaire to an online female writing group as well as writers who identified themselves as females. The questionnaire was also send to friends and acquaintances. Friends and acquaintances were encouraged to send the questions to their writing friends and acquaintances. She put questions on HARO (Help a Reporter Out) website. The responses were classified into internal and external causes. Below are her findings. This finding divided the respondents experiences into two categories external and internal forces that promote doubt.

EXTERNAL FORCES THAT PROMOTE DOUBT

Rejection

Rejection was the most pronounced feeling most writers who responded to the questionnaire experienced. Even one rejection makes people to start feeling as if they don't have what it takes to be writers. We know theoretically that the publication process is subjective. The choices about what will be published depend on what journals and book publishers want at that time, and what their readers expect. It also depends on how many submissions the publication receives for that edition of their publication. The publication also has space constraints. If we look at this process subjectively we blame rejection on our writing shortcomings. Most of the responds point out that they felt dismayed by the rejection notices. Most of them experienced debilitating emotions and decided not to continue submitting their writings to publishers.

Preferences of the publishing world

In the world of publishing we have the traditional publishing houses and the growing self-publishing industry. Depending on where you look, the statistics for getting traditionally published stand at about 1 to 2%. There are new publishing players such as independent publishers, hybrid publishing and self-publishing. These alternative publishing methods greatly improves the odds of getting your article or book published. If it's print or online literary journals or a myriad of other outlets, you are looking to enter your chances of getting published increase even further. A source of frustration that is expressed over and over was that there is often a disconnect between what is published and what is considered 'good'. As they say history is written by the conquers, the publishing industry also has some gate keepers.

Bias

Publishing industry is known for excluding individuals from communities which are marginalised. This marginalisation is manifested through their hiring preferences of writers and editors which leads to gatekeeping. Gatekeeping in publishing refers to the process of selecting and controlling which content is disseminated to the public. Traditionally, this role has been held by publishers, editors, and literary agents.

On the other hand, gatekeepers play a crucial role in maintaining quality standards, because they are able to filter out substandard work. This helps to protect readers from a flood of low-quality content. They also provide expertise where editors and agents offer valuable feedback and guidance to authors. They also help with marketing and distribution of content effectively because they have the resources to reach a wide audience.

Even writers who have achieved a measure of success, still have to deal with this gatekeepers. Although people form disadvantaged groups face more intense scrutiny beyond what their peers must endure. This is where the rubber heats the tar. After writing with so much time invested the road ahead is not as easy. This is where all the coping strategies you have learned so far comes into play. You will not allow this to stop you in your ambition and dream of being a published author.

One thing that you need to keep in mind irrespective of where you choose to publish is to read the authors guidelines and follow them to the letter. Publishers have a market that they are serving. They accept publication for their audience. Whether they are traditional or other publication houses – they are running a business and they should be able to make money to pay their expenses. Read carefully what market the publication is serving and also what are the requirements of the publisher.

The perception that writing should be easy

Many writers encounter skepticism and misunderstanding about their craft from those closest to them. Family and friends often express doubt about the viability of a writing career, showing little interest in the writer's work. Others, unfamiliar with the writing process, mistakenly believe that producing a book or article is merely a matter of finding time, rather than a demanding skill requiring dedicated practice and perseverance. This misconception is frustrating for writers who understand the complexities and challenges inherent in their work. Even with consistent effort, the creative process remains unpredictable and often demands dedication and a strong mind to get published.

Time from writing to publication

You have control over the pace at which you can write and edit your work. This is because you are the only person involved with this process at this stage. However, when it comes to publishing your work there are too many other people who are involved. Firstly, you are going to designed a cover of your book . That is if you are writing a book. If you are writing an article you are going to have to follow the formatting style of the journal for which you are writing.

You have the editor and the reviewers to deal with. Editors and reviewers have ultimate authority over a manuscript's fate, with editors primarily directing manuscript management and reviewers which is part of manuscript assessment. Editors direct the process by selecting reviewers and making the final decision on the publication of the manuscript. When it comes to reviewers most scientific journals reviewers donate substantial amounts of time and energy and are expected to provide timely feedback to editors for no payment at all. It may sometimes take long for you to get feedback.

Online writing forums are rife with writers agonizing over how long it takes to get a response from agents, editors, and journals. It's not unusual for literary journals to take six months to a year to reply. Magazine editors and book agents might never respond to your pitch. And it can take two years from the time you get an offer of representation from an agent to the time your book is published. This waiting time can kill you if you do not know that this is the case. You will have to learn to wait.

The tough part of writing is that it is done for so many months in private, then submissions can take many months, until the writer feels quite separate from the original work. It's hard to keep up any kind of submitting/publishing momentum because of this. It can become worse after waiting for so long to receive negative feedback.

Negative feedback

It sometimes happens that you get very rude editors who make very harsh comments if you did not take time to follow the submission guidelines. They can make comments such as "you are stupid and you will never make it as a writer". These are the people who can do heart surgery without anaesthesia. Sometimes is because they enjoy hurting people. Or it may also be the case that your manuscript found them on a bad day.

You will think that only novice authors with little experience will suffer at the hands of these rude editors. Even experienced authors sometimes experience this rude treatment. In countries with previous racist histories prospective authors suffer from racial bias of the editors and reviewers. As a reviewer it easy to pick up the fact that the paper or manuscript under review was written by someone with English as a second or even third language. Some reviewer can reject your work with confusing comments such as "your methodology is brilliant but you did not write enough." This kind of comments leave you confused and not knowing what is the next step or how to move yourself forward. It can be likened to the situation when you have written a master's or doctoral thesis, and a reviewer simply comments that the work does not meet the standards expected at that level.

If you experience this type of treatment it sometimes can discourage you to the point of losing interest in writing altogether. We are sharing this information with you to enable you to prepare for these kind of scenarios. Disappointment hits you harder if you did not expect it. I wonder sometimes when I see soccer supporters who go to a game with the expectation that their team must win. They do not factor in the reality that the ball is round, it can go in any direction. They do not accommodate the fact that there are always three possible outcomes in a soccer match, unless it is a cup competition where teams are knocked out. The results can be a draw, a win or a loss.

This is why people fight and are injured or even self-harm themselves when their team loses because to them there is only one possible outcome. Writing can be a lonely journey. I like what many institutions do, by organising writing workshops which helps witters feel that they are not alone.

Isolation

Writing is an individual sport like tennis or golf. It can actually be worse than these sports because at least they have spectators to cheer the players. With writing you do it alone in isolation with nobody knowing what you are doing until you finish. You essentially start alone and finish alone. Its only when you are finished and the work is published that you may get some spectators or fans. What makes the isolation of writing worse is how writers spend months or years working on drafts without feedback. This process leaves a room for negative reflection to flourish. Writing is so solitary and individualistic process which exposes the writer to be vulnerable. Everything rests on the shoulders of the writer, that is the vision and the very words used to construct the book or article. Lack of positive feedback, or some kind feedback, makes the isolation harsher than normal. If you have family members who do not understand what you are doing and cannot see your progress it can become daunting. They may start wondering if what you are doing is worthwhile or even necessary. If you have those who are highly opinionated, they may even start asking you and making comments which are not useful and helpful. This just goes to creating even more isolation. You are working alone and in isolation and on the other hand you have people who cannot support because they do not get it.

So far we have been dealing with outside source of discouragement and challenges. It is easier to deal with outside forces than internal ones. An outside enemy is much easier to deal with as compared to the enemy who is already inside. In the next section we are going to deal with the internal sources of discouragement.

INTERNAL SOURCES OF DOUBT

Writing is not an exact science but it is an art. Science is designed to be objective and while art is subjective and deeply influenced by emotions and opinions. The fact that writing is an art means that it is subjective. As a result, it becomes difficult to know when you are on the right track. There is no universal standard to determine the best and worst writing. This is what complicates the writing process.

Insecurity leading to the submission of the work for publication plagues many authors as they start getting concerned about whether they have succeeded in creating a compelling piece of work that will be accepted and read by many people.

Editors and reviewers exacerbated fears of authors by their comments which are generally not friendly and helpful. People have received comments such as "you do not know what you are doing or even worse you are stupid" Insensitive comments such as these often lead authors coming to the conclusion that they are a failure.

The discussion below should help you to look at yourself in more positive way. It is comforting to know that other authors and artists experience this feeling. It helps to know that you are not alone. Some time you may feel the psychological experience of feeling like a fake or a fraud, despite evidence of your competence and success.

Imposter syndrome

Many authors have written about the imposter syndrome. The imposter syndrome is defined as a subconscious feeling experienced by many successful people no matter what kind of success they achieve. They have a feeling that is not real. It is like they are in a dream. It is only a matter of time before someone finds them out. When that happens whatever they may have achieved will be taken away. And as a published writer they will be dropped by their editor or agent or will never publish again.

Imposter syndrome refers to an internal belief or feeling of inadequacy, despite external evidence of competence or success. People experiencing imposter syndrome often have persistent thoughts and doubts about their own abilities, feeling like a fraud or fearing that they will be exposed as incompetent. They tend to downplay their achievements and attribute their success to luck or other external factors, rather than acknowledging their own skills and hard work. Imposter syndrome can be particularly common among high achievers, perfectionists, and individuals who are entering new or challenging environments.

You need to know that the imposter syndrome is going to haunt you as soon as you make a success of yourself. And the more you succeed the more you have to deal with it.

Symptoms of Imposter Syndrome:
- Self-doubt: Constantly questioning your abilities and skills.
- Fear of failure: Believing you'll be exposed as a fraud.
- Perfectionism: Setting unrealistically high standards for yourself.
- Overachieving: Working excessively to compensate for perceived inadequacies.
- Attributing success to luck: Dismissing your accomplishments as chance or external factors.

Below we look at some of the actors who have confessed to the debilitating imposter syndrome.

Jodie Foster won two Best Actress Oscars for her performances in The Accused and The Silence of the Lambs. Still, Foster was worried she'd be discovered to be a fraud. She said "I thought everybody would find out, and they'd take the Oscar back. They'd come to my house, knocking on the door, 'Excuse me, we meant to give that to someone else".

Lupita Nyong'o won an Academy Award for her best-supporting role in 12 Years a Slave. But she revealed to Time Out in 2016, "I go through [Imposter Syndrome] with every role. I think winning an Oscar may in fact have made it worse. Now I've achieved this, what am I going to do next? What do I strive for? Then I remember that I didn't get into acting for the accolades; I got into it for the joy of telling stories."

Twilight star Robert Pattinson told The Observer in 2015, "In a lot of ways, I'm quite proud that I'm still getting jobs. Because of falling into a job, you always feel like you're a fraud, that you're going to be thrown out at any second."

Overcoming Imposter Syndrome:
While it can be challenging, it's possible to overcome imposter syndrome. Here are some strategies:

- Challenge negative thoughts: Identify and question your self-doubting thoughts.
- Focus on accomplishments: Remind yourself of your past successes.
- Set realistic goals: Break down large tasks into smaller, achievable steps.
- Build a support system: Talk to friends, family, or a therapist about your feelings.
- Practice self-compassion: Be kind to yourself and accept your imperfections.

Another internal source of doubt which can be subtle is to compare yourself to other people.

Comparison with others

In order to feel envy, we need to satisfy three conditions. The first one is that we must be confronted with a person who has a quality, or accomplishment that we have not been able to achieve. The second condition is that; we must desire their quality or success for ourselves. Finally, the fact that we the lack these qualities or success must cause us emotion pain.

Envy is distinct from other negative emotions due to its personal nature. Unlike detached feelings like outrage or injustice, envy is deeply rooted in individual desire and longing.

Often confused with jealousy, envy differs in its focus. Jealousy centers on the fear of losing something already possessed or the apprehension of sharing it with others. In contrast, envy is primarily concerned with acquiring what another person has.

Jealousy is different from envy is that fear of losing one's advantages to others, or sharing one's advantages with others.

Envy can be the writer's disease which can become a vocational hazard for most writers. It will often distract you from your own work. It is capable of keeping you awake at night as you think about the success of others.

It is very easy to compare yourself with other successful people. There is nothing wrong with aspiring to be like the successful people you see and know. Nobody succeeds by mistake or overnight. You don't have to be envious of others but you can desire to be like them.

You need to give credit where credit is due. You come from a different background with its own strengths and weaknesses. That is why you need to be careful when you compare yourself to other people. The most important thing is that you have started your journey. Keep to your lane and keep on doing the right thing every day and you will reach where you need to be.

Do not speak ill of those who have achieved more than yourself and find reasons to discredit them. Admire them and determine to learn what made them successful and see if you follow those steps if they will not lead you in the same path. Work towards your own goals and what you expect of yourself.

Personal Expectations

Having high expectations for oneself is a commendable quality. While it often stems from one's upbringing or innate personality, it's a trait that can also be cultivated. We are not sure where this quality come from.

Some people are born into wealthy families, some are born into academic families. Often you see people coming from these kind of background having no ambition or drive. There are times when people from this background excel in their careers or businesses. But we have seen other individuals who come from environments of abject poverty rising and becoming great in life.

It's crucial to maintain a healthy balance between ambition and self-compassion when setting expectations for our writing. While aspiring to make a significant impact is commendable, unrealistic or excessive goals can lead to overwhelming pressure and hinder our creative process. By cultivating reasonable expectations, we empower ourselves to produce our best work without succumbing to self-doubt. Remember, progress, not perfection, is the key to sustained growth and fulfillment as a writer.

Perfectionism

Understanding the source of perfectionism is essential in managing it. Often perfectionism is driven by the desire to avoid failure or harsh judgment and therefore create internal pressures. Perfectionism has a negative aspect which are not helpful. Check if you have the following perfectionist tendencies:

Do you set unrealistically high expectations for yourself and others?

Are you quick to find fault?

Are you overly critical of the mistakes of others?

Do you find yourself procrastinating project out fear of failure?

Do you shrug off compliments and forget to celebrate your success?

Do you find yourself looking to specific people in your life for approval and validation?

Perfectionism if not checked can delay us and almost cripple us as we will not be able to move forward unless all our ducks are in a row. When you have edited your work using all available electronic tools then it is time to send the work forward. Mistakes can always be corrected later. We are not perfect human beings so we will not be able to produce flawless work. Writing is personal and makes us vulnerable.

The personal and vulnerable nature of writing

As we have already mentioned in several times so far, self-doubt has a way of haunting those who want to give their inner self to the world. Writing is one of those things which reveal our vulnerabilities. Wring like any artistic expression is personal and it makes us vulnerable. Vulnerability carries with it the idea of risk. This maybe social risk or economic risk.

It seems with writing the risk is mostly based on the fact that people may shame us, ridicule us. This maybe the reason why some peoples' greatest fear is pubic speaking. I remember when I was in high school as chairperson of the debating team. I was tasked with the responsibility of organising the debate and to enroll the student who were going to debate on the said day of the debate. Students who were chosen to debate had no choice but prepare for the debate based on the topic of the that week. It was during the debate where you saw people being overtaken by fear. This one time I scheduled this particular young man and he begged me not to. But as it was my duty to do so, and the idea was that as many students as possible should be given the opportunity to appear on stage. The guy out of obligation appeared on the stage and he froze. His tongue got stuck in his mouth.

We had to help him off the stage and resuscitate him. We nearly saw trouble that day. Some people do not want to write due to this matter of vulnerability. You have the drive and the ambition, so you are willing to be vulnerable. This has also something to do with how people perceive themselves.

Low self-esteem

Self-doubt is not specific to being a writer. The sad reality is that the majority of us have been brought up in negative parenting atmospheres. We do not have confidence as romantic partners, friends and even workers. Some of us suffer insecurities about our bodies which spills over into other areas of our lives. It is sad that most of us are not where we could have been in life, if we had better parents. Your estimation of yourself determines the degree to which you will doubt yourself in different areas of life, writing included. If you allow your low self-esteem to determine your feelings about yourself, it will distract you from your mission. It will affect your writing ability and output by taking the focus away from your craft. You may find yourself focusing on your ego instead of on the writing process.

It is true that you cannot achieve above your own self-esteem. It seems to be a harsh reality, but it true that we deserve what we have in life. You are where your faith has allowed you to be. You cannot grow above your faith. There is a section later on in this book where we deal with this question of faith in details.

Believe in yourself and your abilities and continue to do things which will helps you increase yourself-believe.

WHAT HELPS, WHAT DOESN'T

If your lack of confidence in your writing is determined by things over which you have no control– such as how long it takes to get responses from editors and agents or what the marketplace favours or any number of other externals – complaining against them probably will not help. A possible exception to this rule includes speaking out against policies or systems that are detrimental to discriminating against certain groups of writers, which can help turn the tide of systemic abuse.

But if your self-doubt is caused by internal forces, there are a number of ways you can work to change your perspective. In the next section we are pointing out the things you can do to take yourself forward. Look at these principles and apply them to see progress. Sometimes our problem is not ignorance but lack of application. Action is what is required for progress!

Unlearn Perfectionism

We discussed perfectionism in an earlier section above. For more information, you can look up that section. However, what we want to re-emphasise in this section is that if you wait for your book or article to be perfect before you send it to the publishers for review you will likely never send it. The other side of the coin is that when you think that you have reached perfection and you send your work and it is rejected then you will be devastated.

With perfectionism - tails you lose, heads you lose. We are born with different degrees of perfectionism and if you have the extreme tendency it will help you to gradually unlearn it. An even interesting one is if you are a reviewer of other peoples work, you are likely not going to be helpful to anybody, because you will find yourself criticising the work of others harshly.

It is not fun to live with a perfectionist, as a matter of fact people with strong leanings towards perfectionism will have very few friends and may find themselves enjoying life less. Let perfectionism not stop you from submitting your work. We need to differentiate between a perfectionist and being cruel as the two can be easily confused. A cruel person has the following attributes : Cruel people **have an intent to harm, because** cruelty involves a deliberate desire to inflict pain, suffering, or emotional distress on others. Cruel people generally lack empathy or understanding of others' feelings. Perfectionism may stop you from submitting your work because you fill it is not yet good enough.

Submit more.

It is an irony that the cure for more or your work being rejected is that you should submit more. After a rejection read the comments carefully and find the courage to help you with your next submission. Never allow rejections devastate you to the extent that you decide never to submit again.

To overcome the disappointment of negative responses, the key is to keep submitting your work. It may be hard to believe when you're still feeling the sting of rejection, but the truth is that the more you submit, the higher your chances of receiving acceptances. It's important to recognize that publishing is a numbers game, and timing can also play a role. Factors like the news cycle can determine what gets published, so understanding these dynamics is crucial.

As part of growing up and developing a strong mind you learn to accept the things over which you have no influence. The time the editor takes to look at your work is out of your control. You should focus on the things you can influence. You have control over the quality of work you produce. You can give a positive spin to the rejections you get. Instead of seeing them as rejection see them as a sign and an opportunity to submit your work to another publisher.

It is standard experience for anybody who wants to publish to have their work rejected by publishers not once but many times. Because you know this, it not going to take you by surprise when your work is rejected. It will hurt when it happens to you for the first time. But because you know in advance that, that is part of the game of publishing. This knowledge should cushion the blow for you.

Sarah Gribble in her blog called the 'Write Practice' gives five reasons why you should aim for hundred rejections. That is, expect your work to be rejected 100 times. Her first reason is that rejections are not failure. You will know that receiving a rejection is painful. We are obviously not going to tell you to rejoice. Getting any sort of literary rejection letter hurts. All of us who have published know the pain. And it does get better every time you get that rejection letter. Remember you can only get a rejection because you submitted your work. You have done something millions have not even tried. It means you tried and you keep on trying. You will thank yourself later for having obtained these rejections because they are going to help you get better as a writer. It means that you are disciplined to finish a project once you start and that is why you are able to get the critique and feedback. It means that your bold as a lion! You should see it as sign of achievement, because it not an indication of failure.

Her second reason for having as your goal to receive 100 rejections is that the you increase the probability of more acceptances. When you are at rock bottom, the only way is up. You cannot go any further down. After receiving that much amount of rejections the chances of more acceptances has just increased. Because you set yourself a goal of a hundred rejections, you will most probably get more acceptances than you would have otherwise obtained. When you have set yourself the goal of rejections it makes you bold and unafraid. This will encourage you to look for publications and submit as much as possible because you do not dread rejections. If you experience failure and you do not give up, it means you understand failure is not final. Setting the goal for a designated number of literary rejection is significant because it means that you are going to have to submit as many articles or books as the envisaged number of rejections. We need to keep in mind that writing is subjective. Setting even a low number of acceptances may seem too ambitious. Remember you have no control over what an editor likes or what mood he may be in on that day. Neither do you have control over who the editor is, and how many of them will look into your work.

She mentions the third reason as being the fact that rejections can be a form of motivation. So the rejection should spur you on to write instead of discouraging you. Because you are aiming at hundred rejections you should have a form of record where you keep the rejection letters. They should be a motivation for you to keep on writing in order to reach the quota of rejections you have set yourself. It is not going to be easy to see these rejection letters but we want them to strengthen your resolve that you are not going to give up. Once you aim for a hundred rejections it means that you will write twice more than the previous years. You can only get an acceptance letters if you keep on writing and submitting. You can only grow as writer if you do not allow rejections to discourage you but instead use them as a means of motivation.

The prospect that rejections will improve your writing is the fourth reason why you should aim for the hundred rejections. In most publication editors will tell you what is wrong with your work and never anything about how you could do to improve it. But some publications encourage their editors to be more helpful. These are the publications which view the review process as developmental tool. The editors may help in the following ways:

- how to make the work more relevant to the journal and to the discipline.
- how you to improve the style and structure of the work to make sure it is communicated effectively.
- provide a critique of the validity, significance, rigor and originality of the work to be published.
- judge how the author could improve their methodology.
- how they could improve the accuracy of the data formuli, quotations, references or figures.
- they present how the author could improve the way they interpret their data sources or references.
- how authors could rephrase or improve the accuracy of their arguments and claims.
- make sure the author does not overstate or understate the significance of their research findings.
- how the author could consider or reference other major publications in their field to make sure the author fully articulates the context of their research and the specific contribution they have made to their field.
- help critically evaluate the accuracy and trustworthiness of research outputs.
- Assist in detecting technical and stylistic flaws within the manuscript, determining the novelty of the study.
- making a recommendation(s) of acceptance, rejection, or revision of the article.
- They examine technical attributes as well
- Verify the scientific quality, clarity of presentation, and ethical validity.

The last reason to aim for 100 rejections is to improve your mind-set. You set yourselves goals because you believe they are achievable. When you have set yourself the goal of one hundred literary rejection letters it helps to soften the blow for every rejection. When you are a new writer you obviously do not know that rejection is part of the game. As you have not personally encountered such experiences, it is possible that you may not be emotionally prepared. However, we hope that you now understand the significance of being mentally prepared to handle such situations.

Find Your Allies

No man is an island. As they say, birds of the further flock together. It has been established that in order to be good at anything in life you need to associate yourself with like-minded people. Now that you want to be a good published writer it means that you need to acquaint yourself with people in the writing world. Check in your country and your town or village if there are writing clubs. In the modern technological era you are not limited to your country only you can join online writing clubs. A simple google search will give you more than enough options.

Working in isolation can be demoralising. Writing is already a lonely process, do not make it worse by choosing to isolate yourself. Reading books on writing may prove to be helpful as you get good ideas on how to hone your craft. If you know an author in your community, why not make contact with them. Often you will find that authors are very friendly people who like to help others.

You should also be available if you are called upon to mentor young upcoming authors through sharing your experience of where you are and where you believe you are headed to.

We hope that having found people who like writing like yourself will help you to pursue your goals even if you come across impediments. In your discussion with other authors they would most probably share with you how they have overcome hurdles put on their way by ignorant people. As you celebrate your victories, remember this is your own journey. But it is good to know that while you are on own your own but you are not alone! That there are people who can be real allies in this creative lonely writing space. You have to find a way to find these allies.

Get a mentor

The most accomplished athlete in various sports have coaches. Sometimes people tend to think that if one is the best in their field they do not require a coach. In this section we are going to dispel that myth and show you that you need a coach. We will refer to coach as mentor. Mentor has five roles they play in lives of those they are mentoring . These are being a teacher, organiser, competitor, learner, and a friend. The fundamental responsibility of the coach/mentor is to help their mentee to reach the highest levels of their performance, which they would otherwise not reach without a coach/mentor. Mentors create the right conditions for learning. They also need to know how to motivate their mentees. The mentorship process requires a myriad of skills for the mentoring process to be effective. Mentors should a have good grasp of the learning processes, teaching methods and training principles. Communication is the at the heart of the mentoring process.

Let us look at the five e roles systematically.

Teacher—The first thing which come to mind when we talk about a mentor is their role as a teacher. This is the area where mentors use their knowledge and skills to prepare their mentees. One of the often neglected skill which is outside the technical skill mentors teach are the psychological skills. These are skill such as mental imagery or relaxation techniques to help the mentee learn and perform new skills. They also train on strategies to help them improve their self-confidence. Control of arousal and anxiety levels is another area in which mentors train. Sometimes the difference between winning and losing depends on the degree to which individuals are able to control their anxiety levels.

Organiser—There is a lot of work that the mentor does behind the scenes. This the organisation of mentoring session which include the scheduling and planning to make for a successful mentoring program. Organisation is necessary aspect for the achievement of success. A mentor must have a clear mentoring plan or what is sometimes referred to a vision, for his mentee. Mentoring is not a haphazard process or trial and error process. Every mentoring session will begin with outlining the steps necessary to achieve success. Mentors are always aware that they are working within time and resource constraints.

Competitor—Mentoring is an emotional process. Mentors are naturally competitive and that is why they have the passion to mentor. They want success. Your writing mentor wants to make sure that you succeed. Your success becomes their success and vice versa. Sometimes mentors do group mentoring.

Learner—A mentor is an ever learning individual. They never sit on their laurels because they want to improve their abilities as a mentor. They experiment with new skills and techniques. They are generally well and broadly read. They are curios human beings. They are on a mission of forever improving.

Finally, they are a friend. Mentors develop strong relationships with their mentees which culminates and takes on the role of a friend. They become a strong positive role model. They are always busy discussing problems, sharing successes, offering support when needed. They also play the role of a counsellor when required. This aspect of mentoring may impact the feelings of satisfaction with the mentor-mentee relationship. This may have a strong positive or negative effect on the mentee. Research has demonstrated that popular mentors want to see improvement of the life of the mentee both inside and outside their work or profession. The writing mentor wants you to succeed in your writing and in life in general. We suggest that you actively go out of your way to look for a mentor.

Take a cue from professional athletes: Having someone in your corner can be a game-changer. Consider it an investment in your career.

Don't Let Fear Drive you

"*Success is not final, failure is not fatal: it is the courage to continue that counts.*"
―― Winston S. Churchill

Fear of failure like any other thing develops slowly from observing people around you. People instinctive avoid failure, because no one wants to fail. In many communities you become a laughing stock if you fail. Fear of failure refers to the inner fear of an individual when he or she perceives that he or she may not achieve a certain goal. The fear of failure is the opposite of the desire to succeed and the motivation to avoid punishment for failure. For most people, fear of failure is uncontrollable. Individuals are often affected by fear of failure and adopt the behaviour of avoiding setting goals, if they cannot be guaranteed of success. The fear of failure is only one thing that makes a dream impossible to achieve. Fear of failure is closely related to uncertainty and risk aversion. Maya Angelou cautions that we will encounter many defeats, but will we must not allow ourselves to be defeated. She further argues that some defeats are necessary as they help us to know ourselves better. These defeats will help us to know what we can rise from, and how you can still stand after being knocked down.

Where there is fear of failure there can never be progress. Fear and success are polar opposite of each other.

Uncertainties may lead to hesitation and procrastination where you find yourself loosing precious time of focusing on your writing. Another way in which fear of failure of may manifest itself is through risk aversion. Generally, risk aversion and fear of failure have a symbiotic relationships. Risk aversion is directly proportional to fear of failure. Being a writer is akin to being an entrepreneur. Entrepreneurs always do risk analyse and wisely to choose moderate risk. Fear of failure is a risk and obstacle to progress. Before you embark on writing as a career or past time you were going merrily bye. Becoming a writer means that your life style is going to change. Writing if done well may change your life completely. It will create another income stream and even end up being your means of living.

Some research has demonstrated that fear of failure had a greater negative impact on female entrepreneurs. It is a pity that some potential writers would not start writing because they were afraid of various risks brought about by the business of writing.

You must not let fear of failure deter you from embarking on the writing voyage. If you do, this will rob you of the views that you may never be exposed to, which only those who are in the ship can see and experience. Life does not stop because you are afraid to fail, others will try and succeed.

If you are going to succeed in your writing, failure is going to be part of that process. People who succeed are those who are who act despite their fears. The more you act, the less you are going to be afraid. The only way of dealing with failure is to do what you have to do.

"I have not failed. I've just found 10,000 ways that won't work."
—— Thomas A. Edison
Let us conclude this section with the apt words of Randy Pausch:

"The brick walls are there for a reason. The brick walls are not there to keep us out. The brick walls are there to give us a chance to show how badly we want something. Because the brick walls are there to stop the people who don't want it badly enough. They're there to stop the other people."

Be a good literary citizen

John F. Kennedy famously said to the American people that they should not ask what their country can do for them, instead they should ask what they can do for their country.

Robert A. Heinlein defined citizenship as an "attitude, a state of mind, an emotional conviction that the whole is greater than the part and that the part should be humbly proud to sacrifice itself that the whole may live."

Reach out to new writers. Help to facilitate the formation of a writing group or join an existing one. Make it your responsibility to help beginner writers as they find their bearings in the writing world. Make sure that the kind of advice you give is solid and helpful to other writers.

WHAT CAN YOUR WRITING DELIVER?

While seeking answers to the question of what causes writers to experience doubts, another crucial inquiry emerged: What are our beliefs about the impact of writing and publication on our lives? What narrative do we hold in our minds regarding how our writing will shape us and our existence?

For some writers, such as Mimi Jones Hedwig, who was an editor , it is the desire to see her work open a dialogue with like-minded readers and have them engage with her characters and worldview. For too many others of us, it is some version of, If I could only get published, then I would be happy. It is this latter narrative that can put untold pressure on our work and heighten our self-doubt.

Writing and publishing are, at best, uncertain undertakings. There are no guarantees, there is much out of our control, and many – if not most who have had great publishing success are still prone to feelings of self-doubt and insecurity. Writing and publishing can be deeply fulfilling endeavours, but they are never a cure-all for what ails us. So get really clear about what your definition of "success as a writer" is. Know what you are demanding from your work. And ask yourself (honestly), "Is this something I can actually deliver?" If not, what can it deliver? It is always better to want what you can have than what you cannot.

Doubt never leaves us alone but is a constant companion. The best in their trade in every life endeavour will tell you that they develop sweaty palms before any performance. Some have even suggested that we should embrace doubt and not see it as an enemy but a companion which keeps us on our feet. We should use the energy of doubt to propel ourselves forward instead of allowing it to be a stumbling block.

The first step of harnessing doubt as a positive energy is to accept and acknowledging that doubt is inevitable. The fact that you have doubt means that you are a writer and does not mean that you are deficient, weird or broken.

Remember this great advice: "you cannot edit an empty page." Even if you feel doubt, continue to write. You may think that doubt is telling you to quit. Stumbling blocks are not there to stop you from achieving your goals, but it is a test to see how much you want to achieve your goals. Believe that the purpose of doubt is to tell you that you are on the right track. So continue writing.

The second step is giving yourself permission to write even though what you write does sound great. It may mean at this point that what you are writing may seem to be wrong. Sometimes you may feel lost in your writing and you may not be able to see how the piece you are writing is connected to the rest of your work. Keep writing because you will have the opportunity to come back to this part. Maybe you may need to delete it or improve on it. You can only correct what is written.

Writing is about putting words on paper. In the writing business, words are never wasted. Although you may not use certain words after writing them, or even though you may have to delete some words, still that is not a waste. All the the words you put on paper strengthens you as a writer. When you keep on writing, you are not practicing bad writing but you are just practicing writing. In the Bible there is a portion where the apostle Paul says some people preach the gospel from envy in order to get him into trouble and yet others preach from a good motive. He concludes by saying either from a good motive or a bad motive but Christ is preached. If you keep going, you will improve even though your writing does not make sense to you at that time.

Now we come to a very interesting step, step three which is about the choice to believe a truth you cannot see. This is what is known as faith. People sometimes like to confine faith to religion. Once they hear the word faith, they immediately associate it with religion. If you are Bible reader, you have come across a very interesting concept pertaining to faith. In more than one instance, Christ has said to some individuals after he heals them, that your faith had made you well. Some of these characters would not even know who Christ was or where he was from. And interesting enough he does not say to them, I am the Christ, I am healing you. Instead he says to them go your faith had made you well. So faith means that you chose to believe in something you cannot verify at that moment.

There will be times you can verify it: good reviews or responses from beta-readers, good moments when you write something and know it is just right, great moments with your writing group in which they understand exactly what you were trying to say. During those times, you can see the truth: you are a writer, and you are getting better, and if you keep going, the story you're trying to tell will take shape.

When doubt hits, you cannot see that truth. When a writer's doubt dogs your heels, bites your neck, hides the sun, you can't even feel that truth. That's the moment to hold onto it—even though it doesn't feel real anymore.

The Writer's Manifesto
Below is the writers manifesto you can adopt and use when days are dark.

I will write when I don't feel like it.
I will write when it hurts.
I think I can write, even if I suck a lot.
People want to read what I write. I know because I want to read it, too.
It's okay if I suck right now. I will figure it out and get better.
I will not stop writing.

The doubt will pass. It will also return. If you hang on to these three steps, you'll make it through.
"

Writing is finally about one thing: going into a room alone and doing it. William Goldman

Tweeted this Tweet:

"Facing the Ugly Truth and Winning

Step one: accept the ugly truth that you will never get rid of your doubt. That means being prepared for its coming.

Step two: give yourself permission to write awfully when the doubt comes. Do NOT listen to the doubt and stop writing. Writing terribly is far better than not writing at all; bad practise is better than no practice.

Step three: Believe that you are a writer and that this time of doubt will pass and that being a writer is worth the fight.

It's that simple and that hard.

It is also worth it. If I can do this, you can. We are in this together, as fellow writers. The doubt will return, but that doesn't mean you have to let it win."

The journey of unleashing the writer within and overcoming self-doubt is not an easy one, but it is a journey worth taking. The key lies in persistence and commitment. Even when you don't feel like writing, push through and write anyway, because that's when the magic can happen. Embrace the pain and use it as fuel for your words, for it is in those moments of vulnerability that your writing can truly touch others.

Remember, it's perfectly fine if you feel like you're not good enough right now. Writing is a skill that can be honed and improved over time. What matters is your determination to keep going, to keep learning, and to keep growing as a writer. Believe in the power of your words, because if you want to read what you write, there are others out there who want to read it too.

Embrace the fact that doubts may arise from time to time. They are a natural part of the creative process. But hold on to these three steps: writing despite the doubt, embracing your imperfections, and never giving up. By following these steps, you will weather the storms of self-doubt and emerge stronger and more resilient.

So, keep writing. Keep putting your thoughts, emotions, and stories into words. You have a voice that deserves to be heard, and through writing, you have the power to make an impact. Trust in yourself, persevere through the challenges, and know that as you continue on this writing journey, you will find your voice, improve your craft, and create something remarkable.

In the end, it is not about being flawless; it's about the courage to try, to learn, and to grow. You have the ability to inspire, entertain, and connect with others through your words. Embrace the journey, embrace the process, and embrace the writer within. You have what it takes to make it through, and your voice deserves to be shared with the world.

CONCLUSION

Self-doubt often accompanies artists, and the art of writing, much like other creative endeavors, is more akin to art than a precise science. Since we cannot completely eliminate doubt from our lives, it becomes necessary to coexist with it without allowing it to overpower us or dictate our actions. Throughout this book, we have provided you with tools and perspectives to contemplate self-doubt and discover methods to manage it effectively.

CHAPTER SIX

BEHAVIOURISM

Theories of Behaviour

Theories of behaviour are important in helping us understand and predict our actions and other people's actions and what influences them. Theories offer a structured framework that aid us in understanding what lies below the behaviours that we see. In this chapter we are going to deal with one of the theories of behaviour namely, behaviourism, which is one of the essential theories in psychology. We will explore how it provides a systematic approach to analysing behaviour, focusing on observable actions rather than internal thoughts or feelings. This chapter will examine the origins, principles, and applications of behaviourism. By understanding behaviourism, we will gain valuable insights into ways in which behaviour can be understood, modified, and applied in various real-world contexts and particularly to us who endeavour to become writers.

History of Behaviourism

Behaviourism emerged as a dominant force in psychology during the early 20th century, marking a departure from the introspection-based methods that previously prevailed. Its roots can be traced to the groundbreaking work of **Edward Thorndike**. Thorndike introduced the **Law of Effect**, a foundational principle in behaviourism. This law suggests that behaviours followed by positive results are more likely to be repeated, while those followed by unpleasant consequences are less likely to recur. Through his experiments with animals, primarily cats in puzzle boxes, Thorndike observed how these creatures learned to escape by gradually eliminating ineffective behaviours.

While Thorndike's work laid the groundwork, **Ivan Pavlov** made significant contributions through his research on **classical conditioning**. Although not a behaviourist himself, Pavlov's experiments with dogs demonstrated how a neutral stimulus (a bell) could be associated with a biologically stimulus (food), leading to a conditioned response (salivation). This discovery provided crucial insights into how learning occurs through stimulus-response associations.

Building upon the work of Thorndike and Pavlov, **John B. Watson** is often credited as the founder of behaviourism. He advocated for a purely objective psychology that focused exclusively on observable behaviour, rejecting the study of mental processes as unscientific. Watson's **stimulus-response (S-R) psychology** emphasized the importance of environmental factors in shaping behaviour. His famous "Little Albert" experiment demonstrated how fear could be conditioned in humans.

B.F. Skinner expanded the behaviourist tradition through his development of **operant conditioning**. Skinner introduced the concept of reinforcement, which involves strengthening behaviour by following it with rewards or removing unpleasant stimuli. His work with rats and pigeons in operant chambers, or Skinner boxes, demonstrated the powerful effects of reinforcement on shaping behaviour. Skinner's emphasis on environmental incidents and the importance of observable behaviour solidified behaviourism's influence on psychology.

While behaviourism has faced challenges and criticisms over the years, its principles continue to be applied in various fields, including psychology, education, therapy, and organizational behaviour. The focus on observable behaviour and the experimental methods pioneered by behaviourists have had a lasting impact on the scientific study of human and animal behaviour. Understanding the principles how behaviour is influenced will help us understand our own behaviour better.

Respondent Behaviour

Respondent behaviours are those over which animals have little control over. These behaviours result from the stimulus that comes before the resulting behaviour. They are also called reflexes. Activities such as seeing or smelling may cause the creature to behave in certain predictable manners. Food may cause the organism to salivate. Sneezing may occur as a result of feeling cold. Hunger may cause the child to start crying, for example.

Respondent behavior, or classical conditioning, significantly influences individuals and society. Involuntary responses to stimuli can shape our emotions, physiology, and memory, impacting personal well-being and decision-making. On a larger scale, these responses contribute to social norms, group dynamics, and cultural practices. From developing phobias to shaping consumer behavior, the effects of respondent behavior are pervasive. Understanding these processes is essential for addressing emotional challenges, navigating social influences, and promoting positive change.

Operant Behaviour

Operant behaviour results from learning from the result of a particular conduct. Most behaviours cannot be explained as reactions over which the creature does not have control. Skinner was not concerned with mental processes that are difficult to comprehend, such as free will. This led him to begin the work of considering the observable environmental factors. Through this work, he learnt that present behaviour is formed by the consequences that *result from previous* behaviours. He argued that the current stimulus does not determine the behaviour.

These aftereffects forecast the likelihood of whether a behaviour may happen again in the future.

In conclusion, operant behavior plays a crucial role in shaping our decisions and actions by linking our behaviors to their consequences. Through the mechanisms of reinforcement and punishment, this type of learning influences our preferences, habits, and decision-making processes across various aspects of life. Whether it's choosing a healthy meal or making significant life choices, the outcomes of our actions serve as a guide for future behavior. By understanding how operant behavior functions, we gain insight into how our past experiences can predict and shape our future actions, underscoring its importance in human psychology and behavior.

The Skinner Box Experiment

The Skinner Box is a controlled environment used to study animal behavior. Developed by psychologist B.F. Skinner, it's essentially a chamber containing a lever or button that an animal can press to receive a reward, such as food or water.

Operant conditioning is the principle behind the Skinner Box. This type of learning occurs through rewards or punishments for behavior. When an animal presses the lever and receives a reward (positive reinforcement), it's more likely to repeat that behavior. Conversely, if a negative stimulus is introduced after the lever press (punishment), the animal is less likely to repeat the action.

By observing and recording these behaviors, Skinner was able to systematically study how reinforcement and punishment influence learning and behavior.[1] The Skinner Box has been instrumental in understanding how operant conditioning works and has applications in various fields, including psychology, education, and animal training.

Skinner created a more robust concept of stimulus control that clarified Pavlov's early understanding of conditioning. He did an in-depth study of animal behaviour, from which he concluded that what seemed to be an innocent stimulus could actually become a stimulus that affects behaviour and makes animals behave in a certain predictable manner.

Behaviourist Theory Regarding Outward vs. Internal Behaviours

In the study of behaviourism, there has not always been agreement on mental states and mental processes. These are deemed personal episodes. Psychologists realised in their study of both animals and humans that internal mental processes, such as thinking processes and emotions, cannot be measured and studied with ease.

Skinner was of the view that although mental processes and emotions were not directly measurable, there should be a way of including them when analysing behaviours. Although he knew that it is more difficult to measure human internal mental processes, there should be a method to amalgamate these internal factors when studying manifest measurable behaviour.

This consideration led him to develop what was to be called radical *behaviourism*. Subsequently, this *formed* the basis for behaviour analysis. The opponents of the behaviourist perspective stuck to what became known as methodological behaviourism because they did not believe that it was necessary to take the feelings and thought of individuals into consideration in analysing behaviour.

The people who opposed this approach formed a movement called radical behaviourism. These people believed that it is crucial, in order to have a wholesome understanding of all human behaviour, that their thoughts and feelings should be taken into consideration. They believed that this will aid in controlling behaviour variables in the history of the individual and society at large.

Because the thinking process and emotions of individual and are sensitive to the same possibilities as behaviours which can be easily observed, they are therefore worthwhile to be studied.

The degree to which one is sick is an internal private matter because only the sick person feels the extent of their pain. We cannot be ignored the fact that this disease will affect their behaviour. The behaviourist believes that because this sickness is an internal stimulus, it will make certain behaviours less likely to occur. Due to this disease, the person is going to be forced to take medication and most probably not go to work that is if they are employed.

What is behaviour?

The theory of behaviour defines behaviour as any action taken by a person. They further believe that behaviour is shaped by the experiences of the individual on a daily basis. Experiences with others in the environment and internal physiological reactions complete an individual's behaviour. That is why you need to be careful not to just follow your feelings. The way you feel about things today is based on your previous experiences. The experiences that made you happy or sad as a child stay with you into adulthood. That is why sometimes you find yourself sad for no apparent reason. Or, for that matter, you find yourself happy for reasons you cannot explain. This is why you need to be self-aware, as we have explained somewhere in this book.

Behaviour analysts try to closely observe the behaviour patterns that are expected from certain individuals. You can also do this for yourself. Observe yourself in terms of your actions and reactions. One of the best things you can do for yourself is to choose your action and stop being reactive. There are certain established patterns of behaviour that people who live with you observe. There are also other general behaviours that people expect from you. Con artists who swindle people of their money use greed as standard behaviour. They know that most people want to get rich quickly. They will promise you that if you invest a certain amount of money you will get a certain high unrealistic return. Because greed has been triggered, you are blinded and you fail to see that what you are being promised is not realistic. Sometimes people appeal to our sympathy to elicit a certain kind of behaviour. There was a trending video on social media of a man who acted as if he were a cripple. Who would walk with difficulty and even dragging one of his legs? The drivers gave him money because he appealed for their sympathy.

There are also certain behaviours that can be difficult for us to understand if we do not have a background understanding of the situation of a person. You are surprised at certain behaviours of other people. Other people are also surprised by certain of your behaviours.

Operant learning predicts behaviour on the basis of repeated results or outcomes that follow the behaviour. The four things which are considered in operant leaning are the things which motivate a person to act, what comes before the individual reaction and how the person responds, and finally the outcome of the behaviour.

The actions and reactions can be explained by analysing the environment in which they are operating based on the context of that particular individual. The reason why we act and react under certain conditions not complex. This complexity is what we need to find out. Sometimes we tolerate things that we should not. Sometimes we are angry about things that do not have to make us angry. This is also where our temptations come from.

If you are a Bible reader, you may have come across the story in which Jesus Christ was tempted by the devil. You would expect him to give into the temptation given his prior experience of not eating for forty day and nights. He was hungry, in fact, very hungry. The first thing he wanted was someone to give him food. The devil tempts him at his point of need, expecting him, given his background and context, to easily fall for the trick. He tells him to turn the stones into bread. Christ had the capacity and the ability to do that, but he was able to perceive the trick.

We can also do the same; choose our actions instead of letting our circumstances to dictate how we react.

In behaviourism, behaviour is a neutral term. Often in everyday language, we use the word to imply undesirable, difficult, or problematic behaviours such as aggressive reaction, theft, or damage to property. But in reality, the term means any action we take both negative and positive. Behaviour analysts are able to determine if a behaviour will increase or decrease based on the patterns of previous behaviour.

We generally think that in the best of times, when all things are equal, people are likely to make the best possible decisions. The kind that will yield the best benefit and satisfaction to them. This is in accordance with the rational choice theory. This theory assumes that when people are faced with various options, they will choose the option that serves their best interest and purposes. The presumption of the theory is that because human beings know their preferences and constraints, they will apply the full capacity of their brain and meritoriously evaluate the costs and advantages of each alternative available to them. The final decision is expected to be the best selection for that person in their circumstances. It is assumed that human beings are rational instead of emotional beings. And that the reasonable individual has the power, control without being moved by feelings and outside factors. As a result, human beings know what is best for them. Behavioural economics stands at the polar opposite of the rational theory and assert that humans are not rational. Due to this, they are not capable of making good decisions. We make emotional decisions and spent the whole time trying to rationally explain our actions. The truth is that people are emotional. We are easily distracted beings, who rarely take decisions that serve our best interest if we are not careful.

In behaviour analysis, the 4-term contingency framework used to analyse behaviour. Another approach to analyse behaviour and contingencies is the nonlinear approach. The nonlinear constructional approach, used to comprehend behaviour, is the brainchild of Israel Goldiamond. He used this approach to understand behaviour.

In the process of analysing behaviour patterns, what is of utmost importance is understanding the purpose served by the behaviour. We also need to evaluate the consequence for the individual. The question is whether we can predict the results that will help determine whether a behaviour will happen again in the future. Behaviourist theory uses reinforcement to predict the outcome of behaviour.

Reinforcement

Reinforcement ensures that a behaviour increases or becomes strong in the future. Reinforcement is a vital value in applied behaviour analysis. When you do a good thing and people appreciate it, you are most likely to repeat that behaviour because of the good feeling you associate with that behaviour. That is why people like those who appreciate them. I remember a young man whose family I used to visit. I will address this young man as "Mr". One time when we visited again he took his homework and showed it to me together with other accolades he got from school. He even told his father that he was "Mr". When his father objected, he said to his father but he calls me Mr., referring to me. When we recognise and appreciate a behaviour, we are reinforcing it. This is why you have all kinds of price giving within organisations. There is positive and negative reinforcement, which we are going to look at in the next section.

Positive reinforcement

What we discussed at in the previous section is positive reinforcement. Positive reinforcement is what builds and helps people. We should recognise and reward good positive behaviour. In some cases, we encourage negative unfruitful behaviour without being aware. When a child throws a tantrum, we do what the child wants because we do not want the child to become a nuisance and embarrass us. We are inadvertently promoting this type of behaviour. We are reinforcing this kind of behaviour.

This does not mean that positive reinforcement will have the same effect on everyone. It all depends on the background and how they were raised. A child and his mother went together to a prize giving event. This child did not receive a prize among the many prizes that were handed out that night. After the event, the mother expressed her disappointment in her child in that he did not even get one price. She told him that some children even got three out to five awards. The mother was thinking that pointing these facts out to her son would motivate him to do better next time. The child said to her mother "did you realise that we used public transport to get to this event? Did you see the cars of the parents of the children who received the awards?"

Negative reinforcement

Negative reinforcement often has to do with escaping from an annoying or unpleasant situation. Something stops after a person behaves in a certain manner. When people do not appreciate what you do for them and instead complain, you can stop what you are doing for them, and sometimes they become aware that you have been helping them. We must stop complaining if we feed negative behaviours in others.

Seat belts are an interesting example of negative reinforcement. Cars are fitted with a mechanism to beep with an annoying sound when the belt is not on. Many people to avoid this annoying sound put on the belt. Some people may not experience the annoying sound emitted by the sit-belt compared to others.

People's personal preferences, as well as tolerance levels determine whether reinforcement will work or not. People who do not enjoy to be the centre of attention in public, if they decide to share their ideas, for example, in a staff meeting and they receive immense positive attention from colleagues, this may lead them to never talk again in a public meeting. But if someone likes the attention they get from colleagues and they also like sharing ideas in meetings, they will be encouraged to share ideas in a staff meeting whenever an opportunity presents itself. Attention functions differently for different people. It is positive reinforcement for those who like attention in this case and negative for those who do not like attention. As they say, one man's poison, another man's medicine. Something that is positive reinforcement may be negative reinforcement for another person.

Parents who grew up poor and then escaped poverty as a result of hard work. Scarcity has been their motivation. They did everything in their power to avoid being poor. This sometimes gives them wrong ideas as to what to motivate their children who are growing up in the midst of abundance. They wrongly think that because they were motivated by lack and scarcity, their children should be similarly motivated. These parents will then try to deprive their children of the things they themselves did not have, hoping that, that is how their children will be motivated. Unfortunately, this artificially created poor environment cannot motivate their children is fake, it is not genuine. It does not exist.

Punishment

In our modern culture, the concept of punishment is frowned upon. We believe that punishing children will harm them and scar them for life. We equate punishment with trauma and toxic implications. In its nature, punishment is inclusive of discomfort. It is never pleasant to be corrected and admonished. The purpose of punishment is to remove or decrease the unwarranted behaviour that, it does not continue to happen in the future. The purpose of reinforcement is to promote a desirable behaviour whilst punishment aims to diminish the unwanted behaviour in the future.

Positive punishment is always in time and clearly associated with the offence. Punishment takes place when an unwarranted behaviour is immediately followed by the action which has the possibility of reducing the repetition of the behaviour. On the other hand, when punishment is negative, the behaviour is not followed by removing the thing which will lessens the possibility of a similar action given the same conditions immediately.

The behaviour that is tolerated will be repeated. If we complain about a person's behaviour that we do not like and we do not do anything about that behaviour, the person has no reason to change. It is true that we get what we deceive. This is a truth that is bitter but we have to accept it. Nothing will happen if we do not do something. Doing the same thing over and over expecting different results is called madness.

You have to decide what you want and pursue it. Sometimes the problem is that we do not know what we want. The idea in this chapter is that you should understand your own behaviours and those of other people. If you we do not understand our own behaviour and those of others, we are likely to make some wrong decisions in pretext that we are fixing ourselves or the other people. Often we want to change other people, when in reality it is us who need the change. We can give many examples of this mind set.

One lady asked me to help her son, who was not motivated and could not focus and finish any course he registered for. I asked her to tell me more about her son. She explained to me that her does not have post matric qualifications. After matric he got himself a job in the retail industry. He met his wife who was a nurse and they got married. His wife supported him and was willing to sacrifice everything to help him succeed. The wife suggested that he should resign from his job and go back to school so that he could obtain a profession. This was a good idea. He went to college to study to become a teacher. Meanwhile, the wife fell pregnant. The mother of the boy suggested that the girl can take unpaid leave and they will help them in those months that she would not be earning.

The boy failed some modules at the end of the year. And he decided that he was not going to continue with the teachers course as he has lost interest in the course. The mother suggested that he should go to university and study law. His wife agreed. She finished her maternity leave and went back to work. The daughter in law, together with the mother of law, worked together to pay for the young man for his law degree. He passed his first year course. In his second year, he did not do very well. He decided not to return to university because he found the course boring.

The mother asked me to talk to him and she believed that would may help him focus and complete his studies. If you analyse this situation, you realise that this young man never decides what to do. It is either the wife or the mother who suggests what he should do. He always agrees, but loses interest in the middle of his project. I suggested to the mother that the people who can help this situation are the wife and the mother, as they perpetuating this situation.

My advice to her was to explain to her the concept of negative and positive punishment and reinforcement.

Behaviour analysts prefer positive reinforcement strategies against punishment. These strategies have the effect of improving the kind of behaviours we expect compared to the use punishment to restrain the unwanted behaviours. Reinforcement has shown to result in longer-term success. As an author, it will help you identify the things which reinforce your positive actions. As a writer, sometimes you feel that you are not making the kind of progress you think you should be making. During this time, you have to pull from your memory bank that have helped you with motivateyou in the past. Recall the reason why you are writing. Recall your success. If you do not remind yourself of this good things regularly, you may forget. This leads us to another behavioural principle known as extinction.

Extinction

Extinction refers to a situation where a previously reinforcing behaviour no longer produces the same reinforcement. This is the third principle together with punishment and reinforcement. If reinforcement is withheld the frequency of the behaviour may be cutback, this is what we refer to as extinction.

Sometimes we need to be careful of how much we depend on other people for our motivation. People are sometimes happy and sometimes are unhappy. It is good to take the good we get from others and use it to our good. The only danger is when we are not sufficiently motivated and our main motivation comes only from the outside. It is easy to experience extinction, if these people we have been relying for motivation have other days or are just too busy. We need high levels of self-motivation and intrinsic motivation and self-reliance. You should be able to believe in yourself even if no one believes in you for whatever reason. Extinction is a very real danger for anybody who want to achieve goals beyond your peers or people the immediate environment in which you live.

Reading auto-biographies or biographies of pioneers and high achievers sometimes help. When reading these stories, they will shield us against extinction. Napoleon Hill in his book entitled think and grow rich states that "Failure is a trickster with a keen sense of irony and cunning. It takes great delight in tripping one when success is almost within reach "

In recent times, most behaviourist practitioners prefer more respectful techniques instead of using extinction. These alternatives are safe and socially acceptable. They enable them to maintain good relationships with their clients.

Behaviourist Theory on Functions of Behaviour

The central idea in studying behaviour analysis is to understand the meaning and motivation behind people's behaviours. Ideas such as reinforcement and punishment reveal the motivation behind a behaviour. Behaviour analysis attempts to find that which reinforces the behaviour that is being maintained by the individual. A good behavioural analyst requires the skills of the best detective.

One of the tools used by detectives in investigating crime is motive (*Motive*, n.d.). Motive is often understood to be the reason a person commits a crime. The motive is the impulse that induces criminal action. Detectives combine motive and evidence to prove that a person committed a crime. Evidence can be used to prove Motive. If there is sufficient evidence, a motive may not be necessary to prove a crime. The behaviour analyst observes, measures, and analyse behaviours.

Behaviourists have identified four functions of behaviour. The functions are Automatic, Escape, Tangible and Attention/Social. These four functions work in conjunction with each other. Even though you have four functions which work in tandem, one will stand out as a primary function. Let us discuss these four functions and their implications for understanding our own behaviour and that of others around us.

The automatic function is not socially mediated. The individual engages in the behaviour because it gives them good feelings. The pleasure derived from this behaviour results in a pleasurable sensory experience.

The result of good feelings and sensory experience comes from the voluntary involvement. Engaging in the behaviour just feels good. This behaviour is self-reinforcing, and a person continues to carry out the behaviour for the sake of the behaviour. If you see the people who run daily on our streets, they do it on their own and for no apparent benefit. People who are involved in religious organisation continue to do what they believe the divine wants them to do. They do it regularly and with great commitment.

The next behaviour function is called escape. In this case, participating in the behaviour helps the individual to get or stay out of trouble. If someone is dealing with a boss who shouts too much, the person may choose to keep quiet while the boss is shouting or they may start crying. This will depend on which one has worked for them in the past. They will choose a behaviour that stops or reduces the shouting.

The third behaviour function is called tangible. With this behaviour function, the person will gain something tangible as a result of participating in the behaviour. This may be something like a physical item or an activity. The tangible reinforcement results from this kind of behaviour. Workers have a tendency to time their strikes when there is a significant event knowing that their employees have little wiggle room.

The last behaviour function is known as attention or social. Human beings are gregarious. We always want and enjoy the company of others. We are social beings. Our behaviours are maintained by social attention from others. Unfortunately, this behaviour function does not result only in positive behaviours. Gangsters and criminal syndicates thrive because of the attention and social interaction the members enjoy from each other.

Conclusion

People have their own value systems. There are things that people put a high price on. This differs for one group of people to another. There are also differences between individuals. Behaviour analysis focusses on creating consequential transformations for an individual according to their values. People are helped to improve the quality of their lives without imposing new of foreign values systems. Behaviour analysts, like all professionals in the area of self-development, teach their clients new skills.

People can be taught new and useful skills not because they are doing anything wrong but to improve the quality of their lives. Behavioural psychology often deals with the elimination of problematic behaviour. The discoveries of early behaviourists, such as Skinner influenced the learning theories. Given the history of any branch of science, there are horror stories and atrocities committed by scientists in an attempt to gain deeper understanding of human behaviour.

It may be worth reading about the history of how behaviour analysis was used as a tool for harm rather than good in some cases. It was applied in ways that violated the values and dignity of the people it was supposed to help. There are objectionable methods used in early behaviour modification by people like Ivar Lovaas in his work with individuals with autism.

Fortunately, measures have been built into research dealing with human subjects. There is an imperative to comply with strict ethical principles and practises by all scientist. The good news is that the field has developed significantly in a positive way. The people involved in the research are treated with compassion. The field tries to empower people and create a healthier environment by applying their scientific findings in a companionate manner. Remember that the initial experiments were conducted with animals. Later scientists discovered that the some of the principles like operant behaviour could be useful to human beings. The principles discovered helped to establish behaviour analysis as practiced today. Their theories have improved the quality of life of humans in a small and large way. Science has been applied to influence socially significant behaviour learning and education.

CHAPTER SEVEN

THE PYGMALION EFFECT

There is no argument that the power of expectations raises the performance of individuals. Rosenthal was the first researcher to observe and document this phenomenon among children in classroom settings. It has now been confirmed with adults in diverse organisational contexts. Researchers have consistently found that artificially boosting the expectations of an authority figure (teacher, instructor or boss) regarding the potential of his/her charges, improves the performance of those subjects compared to the control group. This self-fulfilling prophecy has been labelled the "Pygmalion effect".

The Pygmalion effect was first observed in the classroom, but it applies to all areas of life. The Pygmalion effect is also known as the Rosenthal Effect. It is a phenomenon in which the expectations of teachers, mentors, and other influencers can have a significant and measurable impact on the performance of those under their influence. I hope that you can relate to this idea and its effect on you and other people around you. This phenomenon is good if you are on its positive receiving site. It is very bad if you were at its negative receiving site. Bu in one way or the other you will see whether you were in the positive or negative site as we delve deeper in explaining it. It is an important concept in life in general and particularly in education. It can have a powerful influence on student performance and learning.

The Pygmalion Effect is based on the Greek myth of Pygmalion and Galatea, in which a sculptor falls in love with his sculpture of a woman. The myth has a different version. We will not look into all of them in this book. But if you will search the Internet, you find the different versions. We have adopted the version below.

According to Greek mythology, Pygmalion was a king of the island of Cyprus and a sculptor who may have been a human son of the sea god Poseidon. He spent many years carving an ivory statue of a woman more beautiful than any living woman. Pygmalion became absorbed by his sculpture and fell in love with it. He pretended that it was an actual woman. He brought the statue gifts and treated it as if it were alive. Nevertheless, the statue would not respond to his kindness. Pygmalion became miserable. He decided to pray to the goddess of love – Aphrodite, to give him a woman like his statue. Aphrodite did even better. She brought the statue to life. Pygmalion married this woman, often called Galatea. She bore him a beautiful child. Depending on which version of the myth you come across this could have been a son or daughter.

THE PYGMALION EFFECT

The Pygmalion Effect is an incredibly powerful phenomenon that has been studied for decades by psychologists, educators, and researchers. It is a kind of self-fulfilling prophecy. A self-fulfilling prophecy is described as a prediction that causes itself to become true. According to this concept, if we prophesy - that is, expect something to happen in a certain way. We are likely to behave consciously or unconsciously but mostly unconsciously in a manner that will make what we expect to happen. There are two types of self-fulfilling prophecies. The first one is self-imposed prophecies that transpire when our own expectations influence our actions. As an author, this is the kind of prophecy you need because you are in control of it. This is what is sometimes referred to as intrinsic motivation. The second one is the prophecies imposed by others which arise when the expectations of others influence our behaviour. All opinions you value can cause this prophecy. We will knowingly or unknowingly do everything in our power to make sure our prophecy becomes true. It has been found to have a profound influence on student achievement. Pygmalion Effect is based on the idea that expectations can have a powerful influence on behaviour. If a teacher or mentor has high expectations for their students, those expectations can actually cause the student to perform better and achieve more. This means that experimenters unwittingly influence the results of their research. The experimenters refer to people on whom others depend, such as physicians, therapists, employers, teachers, and so on. This conclusion raises the nature/nurture controversy and disputes about the malleability of intelligence. Pygmalion confirms the power of environmental on the individuals' thinking behaviour and achievements of people. The main emphasis of Pygmalion is the effects of teacher expectancy on academic performance rather than intelligence.

The Pygmalion effect also applies to both positive and negative expectations. If a teacher or mentor has low expectations of their students, those students are more likely to perform poorly and will likely not meet the expectations set for them. However, if a teacher or mentor has high expectations of their students, those students are more likely to perform better and meet the expectations set for them.

HISTORY OF THE PYGMALION EFFECT

The concept of the Pygmalion effect was first studied in the 1960s by a team of psychologists led by Robert Rosenthal at Harvard University. The team conducted a series of experiments that showed that expectations can have a strong influence on student performance. In one experiment, they showed that when teachers were told that certain students were bright and likely to excel, those students ended up performing better than those who were told that they were not as bright.

Robert Rosenthal and school principal Lenore Jacobson conducted a study in which they told school elementary teachers that on the basis of some psychological tests some of the children in their class were designated as late bloomers even though they had not shown any academic success they are expected to bloom.

The experiment took place in the elementary school in a run-down section of a middle-sized city of South San Francisco. About 17% of the students were Mexican, the only minority group in that city. For each of grades 1 through 6, there were three classrooms because the school used an ability-tracking system that placed children in a slow, medium, or fast classroom depending on their scholastic performance.

In May 1964, the teachers were asked to administer a test to all children in grades K through 5. Each teacher administered the test to his class. However, the teachers were not told the true name of the test, instead, they were told it was a test from Harvard University that predicted academic 'blooming' or "spurting" by most of the pupils who performed well on the test. For the elementary grades there are three

Although the experimenters were interested in raising the intellectual level, teachers were apparently told to expect academic blooming. Additionally, each teacher was given an information sheet explaining that the primary interest of the Harvard study of inflected acquisition, was supported by the National Science Foundation. The test was supposed to pick children expected to show an unusual forward spurt of academic progress within the next year or less. At the same time, the study was supposed to provide a final validity check on the new test's ability to pick out these children. The pre-test consisted of 305 children in the control group and 77 in the experimental group. The timetable for two of the three future testing sessions was disclosed to the teachers (Spitz, 1999).

The teachers began to treat those children differently than the other kids. Those kids began to think of themselves differently and in the end they actually performed significantly better than the other kid. According to this experiment, the children were transformed by the positive expectations. In other studies, in which teachers had a negative expectation of their students, they thought of themselves as inferior. These students under-performed as a result of the teacher's low expectation.

Robert Rosenthal and school principal Lenore Jacobson took the Pygmalion effect one step further. Rosenthal opined on the TV show that what they wanted to show was the extent to which teachers' expectations could actually affect the intellectual performance for example their IQ scores. They tested all the children in their experimental school with the Harvard test that they pretended to be a test that would predict academic blooming. They gave each of the teachers in the school the names of a handful of children in her classroom that would get smart in the academic year ahead. These student names were chosen randomly using a table of random numbers. The children did not know directly that the teachers were holding certain expectations of them. Teachers were told not to tell the kids. And the experimenters did not tell the children either. The children never knew. When they were tested a year later it was found that those kids who had been alleged to their teachers to show intellectual gains in fact showed greater intellectual gains than the children of whom nothing was said in particular.

This experiment proved that the kids actually got smarter when their teachers expected them to improve. There are four factors that operate in the mediation or communication of these self-fulfilling prophecies, especially in the classroom. This is confined not only to the classroom but also to other areas of life. Let us look at the four things the teachers do differently to kids for whom they have more favourable expectations.

The first factor is the climate factor. The climate factor (Walterdavis, 2020)is the kind of social and emotional mood that we create for others. According to Rosenthal, when we expect more favourable things from people, we create a more positive interpersonal environment for them. Teachers tend to create a warmer climate both verbally and non-verbally (for example, they will smile more often at them) for those children for whom they have more favourable expectations. They are nicer to them both in terms of the things they say and also in the nonverbal channels of communication. · Providing positive non-verbal cues through tone of voice, eye contact, facial expressions, and body posture or movements crates the positive climate. · Helping an employee or student set challenging goals is another way of creating the positive climate. These are ways to create a positive climate. There is however the negative climate; which are poor behaviours that communicate low expectations. These are things like ·being distracted when dealing with subordinates, being in a hurry or otherwise not giving the subordinates. · Negative climate is created by verbally criticising the competence or potential of the subordinates. There are also negative non-verbal cues through voice, face and body posture or movements (walterdavis, 2020).

The second factor is the so known as the input factor. Teachers teach more material to those children for whom they have more favourable expectations. If you think a kid is dumb and cannot learn, you are not going to put yourself out there trying to teach them much. Rosenthal says: "We teach more to those from whom we expect more.

Spend as much time as is necessary with subordinates and provide them with ideas to follow up on or additional sources of information to use. There is a healthy balance required where the teacher or manager does not usurp ownership of the assignment, but provides enough resources or ideas.

The negative input factor is when we do not give people who depend on us sufficient direction, guidance, or vital information to complete an assignment. Waiting too long to check progress and provide any necessary course correction. Provide very limited information without reason.

The third factor is the response opportunity factor. The kids get more of a chance to respond if the teachers expect more of them they call on them more often. When they call on them, they let them talk longer, and they help shape with them the answers that the kids speak out, kind of working together to put the response out.

The fourth factor is the feedback factor. If more is expected of a kid the kid is praised more positively reinforced more for getting a good answer. The student is given more differentiated feedback when they get the wrong answer. One of the ways in which one can sometimes tell a little bit that the teacher does not have very high expectations for the kid is that the teacher is willing to accept a low-quality response. I could be helpful for the teacher to clarify what would have been a good quality response. This maybe because he/she feels that what is the use; the kids who is not smart enough will profit from this additional clarification.

HOW DOES THE PYGMALION EFFECT IMPACT LEARNING?

The role of managers, teachers, parents, and coaches is huge, they have an immense power to affect performance outcomes. Their expectations of their dependents can send someone to the stars or make nobody out of them. There is saying that the poor become poorer and the rich become richer. We have all seen how children from poor neighbourhoods hardly rise and make their lives better. Often this is because no one believes in them. No one gives them positive messages; they do not get the positive reinforcement of their self-esteem. They have a low level of expectation of themselves. Those of you who follow sport will know the effect a coach has on the team. Great sports clubs are coached by people who have high expectation for their players. These coaches have a way of communicating what they expect by expressing it verbally and through their actions. The Pygmalion effect can have a strong influence on learning. When a teacher or mentor has high expectations for their students, those students are more likely to perform better and achieve more. This is because students are motivated to meet the expectations set for them. The Pygmalion effect can also have a positive effect on the learning environment. When teachers and mentors have high expectations of their students, it encourages them to strive for excellence and gives them the confidence to take risks and explore their potential.

In addition, the Pygmalion effect can also have a positive impact on student behaviour. When students are given high expectations, they are more likely to follow the rules and behave in a positive way. This is because they want to meet the expectations set for them by their teachers and mentors.

THE ROLE OF BELIEF IN THE PYGMALION EFFECT

It is an interesting fact that we teach more to those from whom we expect more. We tend to give them more information to enable them to do a better job. Pygmalion only works if the expectations are real. The Pygmalion effect cannot be faked. It is based on the genuine faith of the mentor in the mentee. The genuine belief that we have in others raises their own self-belief. If you think someone is an idiot, it will not help to tell them that they are a genius, because that is not how it works. This is not wishful thinking.

Whatever you truly believe about the person in front of you, you are sending signals most of them subconsciously, and again on the receiving end subconsciously the other person will integrate those signals and act accordingly. So how can we make this thing work if you have a total loser in front of you or you are the new manager to a losing team in sports or in business or your kid always comes home with bad grades and you start to expect that to happen the next time, what do you do because those expectations will show now you know that and they will reinforce the same outcome over and over again.

Belief is an important factor in the Pygmalion effect. When a teacher or mentor has high expectations for their students, these students are more likely to believe that they can meet those expectations. This belief can then have a powerful influence on their performance.

Belief plays an important role in self-fulfilling prophecies. If a teacher or mentor has high expectations for their students, those students are more likely to believe that they can meet those expectations. This belief can then lead to an improvement in their performance.

Belief is also an important factor in the Pygmalion effect because it can lead to a positive feedback loop. When students believe that they can meet the expectations set for them, they are more likely to work harder and put in more effort. This can then lead to an even better performance, which can then lead to a further improvement in your beliefs.

PYGMALION EFFECT AND FAITH

Napoleon Hill's famous book Think and Grow Rich deals extensively with the question of faith. He argues that faith means convincing yourself that your goal is achievable. Faith works just like the Pygmalion effect except that it works through and can be trained and improved through self-suggestion. When people around you send you positive messages and you start believing in something or have a specific goal in mind, you must practise convincing your mind of the opportunity to achieve that goal. After a while, your mind will start to subconsciously act on behalf of your belief system. In a nutshell, you become what you think about.

Faith is the great equaliser; in many cases, it is the cause of misery and failure, but becoming aware of its power and steering its force toward meaningful goals often makes all the difference in the world (Martina, 2018).

Purposely avoid negative emotions and focus all your energy on positivity; this world is now more abundant than ever, and we have no excuses - none — for not realizing our full potential.

Hill also mentions the importance of writing down your goals, repeating them day in and day out for 30 minutes a day, and promising yourself that you will be relentless in their pursuit. Actually, he suggests a detailed process for injecting both ambition and faith into your goals. This process includes:

- Go to a tranquil place, where you know you will not be disturbed. Close your eyes and repeat your affirmations out loud your affirmations;

- repeat the affirmations every day and night;

- Put a copy of your affirmations in a place where you can see them every day and read them both before going to bed and when you wake up.

However, half-heartedly repeating your affirmations does not make sense; make sure that, while repeating, you can feel and sense your goals as already accomplished. Stretch your imagination to the maximum and put emotion into your thoughts.

If you read the Bible, you come across this interesting phenomenon of faith. Many times Jesus Christ will ask people who come to him for healing: 'What do you want me to do for you?' When they answer him, he says to them very often 'let it be done according to your faith.'

This shows that faith is religious concept although that is where is mostly talked about. But we see that it touches all areas of life.

BENEFITS OF THE PYGMALION EFFECT

The Pygmalion effect can have a number of important benefits for students, teachers, and mentors. For students, the Pygmalion effect can lead to improved performance, increased motivation, and increased confidence. For teachers and mentors, the Pygmalion effect can lead to improved relationships with their students, increased engagement in the classroom, and improved teaching methods.

The Pygmalion effect can also lead to better student outcomes. When teachers and mentors have high expectations of their students, those students are more likely to achieve those expectations. This can lead to better grades, better test scores, and improved overall school performance.

COMMON MISCONCEPTIONS ABOUT THE PYGMALION EFFECT

One of the most common misconceptions about the Pygmalion effect is that it only applies to students. While it is true that the Pygmalion effect is most commonly studied in the context of students, it can also be applied to any other situation where expectations can influence performance. For example, the Pygmalion effect can be applied to employees in the workplace, customers in the marketplace, and even athletes in the sporting arena.

Another common misconception about the Pygmalion effect is that it applies only to positive expectations. While it is true that the Pygmalion effect is most commonly studied in the context of positive expectations, it can also be applied to negative expectations. If a teacher or mentor has low expectations for their students, these students are more likely to perform poorly and do not meet the expectations set for them.

STRATEGIES FOR APPLYING THE PYGMALION EFFECT

The Pygmalion effect can be a powerful tool for educators, mentors, and other influencers. Here are some strategies to apply the Pygmalion effect in the classroom and other learning environments.

1. Set high expectations for your students. Make sure your expectations are realistic and achievable but also challenging enough to motivate your students.
2. Communicate your expectations clearly. Make sure your students understand your expectations and why you have set them.
3. Provide positive feedback and rewards. Make sure that your students are aware that they are meeting your expectations and that they are being rewarded for their efforts.
4. Monitor progress and adjust expectations accordingly. Make sure that you are monitoring the progress of your students and adjusting your expectations as needed.
5. Encourage students to take risks and explore their potential. Encourage your students to take risks and explore their potential, as this can help them to achieve their goals.

EXAMPLES OF THE PYGMALION EFFECT

The Pygmalion effect has been studied in a number of different contexts. Here are some examples of the Pygmalion effect in action:

1. In a study conducted by Robert Rosenthal at Harvard University, it was found that when teachers were told that certain students were bright and likely to excel, those students ended up performing better than those who were told that they were not as bright.
2. In a study by Carol Dweck at Stanford University, it was found that students who received positive feedback on their performance were more likely to persist and achieve their goals than those who received negative feedback.
3. In a study conducted by Robert Zajonc at the University of Michigan, it was found that students who had high expectations were more likely to learn and retain information than those who were given low expectations.

THE INTERPLAY OF THE PYGMALION EFFECT AND SELF-FULFILLING PROPHECY

The Pygmalion effect and self-fulfilling prophecy are closely related phenomena. Both are based on the idea that expectations can have a strong influence on performance. The Pygmalion effect is based on the idea that high expectations can lead to improved performance, while self-fulfilling prophecy is based on the idea that low expectations can lead to improved performance.

The Pygmalion effect and self-fulfilling prophecy can also work together to create a positive feedback loop. If a teacher or mentor has high expectations for their students, those students are more likely to believe that they can meet those expectations. This belief can then lead to an improvement in their performance, which can then lead to a further improvement in their beliefs. This positive feedback loop can then lead to even better performance.

The green circles containing a plus (+) symbol next to every step in the cycle indicate that all the steps of the loop are positive in nature.

The cycle begins when teacher, coach, or manager believe that a particular team member is capable of higher performance. This positive belief influences the behaviour and actions of the subordinate.

If the team member performs well, the mentor should praise them. Otherwise, if there is under-performance, the mentee is gently supported by getting more information about the task, and this action will make them aware that you believe they are capable of much more.

The self-beliefs of the team member will then be influenced positively. This will help them to believe that they are a good performer.

This newfound increased belief that they are a high performer will cause their actions and performance to improve.

Finally, this increased performance will reinforce your belief that the team member is a high performer.

Thus begins a virtuous self-fulfilling prophecy as you go around and around the loop, with your positive beliefs about your team member being reinforced, at the same time as their positive beliefs about themselves increase and so does their performance.

The Pygmalion Effect Explained

The Pygmalion effect is a psychological phenomenon in which higher expectations lead to increased performance.

The Pygmalion Effect gets its name from ancient Greek mythology and the story of Pygmalion, who fell in love with one of his sculptures. Pygmalion is also the name of a play by George Bernard Shaw. The play explores the idea that how you treat another person affects their life, either for better or worse.

The Pygmalion Effect Experiment

The Pygmalion effect was first observed in the classroom, but you can find examples of it everywhere.

The original study observing the phenomenon was conducted in a school in 1968 by social psychologist Robert Rosenthal and elementary school principal Lenore Jacobson.

The study worked by first giving students a test that is said to identify potential intellectual superstars. These were the students who had the highest capacity for academic growth.

The teachers were then provided with the names of these superstars. At the end of the academic year, the students were tested again and, sure enough, the superstars had progressed significantly further than their classmates over the year.

But here is the thing: the superstars were actually chosen at random. The only difference between the superstars and their classmates was in the mind of their teacher!

Therefore, the Pygmalion effect in the classroom experiment showed that high expectations of a child can result in an increase in child performance.

In summary, the Pygmalion effect in classrooms says that if a teacher believes that a child is bright, their expectations and behaviour towards that child will change positively. The child will rise to this higher expectation and believe that they are bright. As a result, your performance will improve, and this will then reinforce the teacher's belief that they were right to have high expectations for the child.

Pygmalion Effect in the Workplace
It turns out that the Pygmalion effect does not just exist in schools; it exists in the workplace as well. If a manager believes that their team consists only of high performers, they will outperform an equivalent team whose manager believes the opposite.

Why is this? Well, because when a team member is treated as though they are a high performer, they try to live up to that image and behave and perform how they believe a high performer would.

The opposite is also true. When a team member is treated as though they have no chance of success, they live up to this expectation and perform poorly.

It turns out that team members tend to do what they are expected to do.

Using the model

The Pygmalion effect gives teachers, parents, coaches, and managers a secret superpower to create a high-performing team and positively impact peole. This is because when you believe people have what it takes to become a great performers, that belief becomes a reality.

There are two facets of the Pygmalion effect that you should understand:

1. Setting your expectations promotes subordinate performance.
2. Managers tend to allocate their time and energy to subordinates in proportion to their expectations.

To use the Pygmalion effect, we want to treat all of our subordinates in a high-quality way, leading to superior performance.

A great subordinate-manager relationship can not only lead to superior performance, but can also increase employee retention. A survey by Ultimate Software found that 58% of employees would turn down a 10% pay rise to stay with a great boss.

Some simple steps that we can take to make use of the effect include the following.

Set challenging but not too challenging goals.

By setting goals specific to them, your subordinate will know what you expect from them. However, to benefit from the Pygmalion effect, goals must be more than just aspirational.

For your subordinate to be motivated by a goal, they must believe that it is realistic and achievable. If you encourage subordinates to strive for unattainable goals, they may well give up trying and deliver inferior performance.

Invest in your own management training.

What you believe about your own managerial ability to hire, train and motivate your subordinates will affect the performance of your subordinates.

If you have genuine confidence in your ability, you will have high expectations of your team and your team will rise and meet these expectations.

But how do you go about increasing your own belief in your ability? One of the simplest ways is to continually invest in your own management training and professional development.

Give positive feedback.

Even your most productive subordinate needs occasional positive feedback on how they are performing.

Your underperformers also need positive feedback. One way to achieve this is to provide positive feedback on an area of their work, such as their effort level, before giving constructive feedback on their underperformance.

Train and coach your people.

You have set goals that will challenge your subordinate to improve their performance. Effort alone may not be enough to increase your performance to the desired level, so you need to ensure that you have the right tools to enhance your performance.

There are many ways you can achieve this, the most common being through training courses, mentoring, and coaching.

Practise high leader-member exchange leadership.

To put it in the simplest possible way, practising high Leader-Member Exchange Theory (LMX) means exhibiting characteristics towards your subordinate such as trust, respect, acting professionally, and displaying loyalty.

The Golem Effect

The Pygmalion effect refers only to the positive case whereby positive expectations lead to increased performance. The opposite case, whereby you place lower expectations on an individual and that, in turn, leads to lower performance, is known as the Golem effect. It is a negative self-fulfilling prophecy. Negative self-reflexion results in poor performance. When you notice poor performance, your negative expectations are confirmed, reinforcing your beliefs even more strongly (*The Pygmalion Effect Explained - Expert Program Management*, 2021).

Organisations depend on managers to produce results. This put managers under increasing pressure to produce results. To get results, they have to get the best from those who report to them. Often, in their attempts to get results, they unintentionally estrange those they regard as lower performers. This kind of action diminishes unit performance, but also because it harms their organisational reputation as coaches. This leads to low morale among staff. Moreover, it can cause considerable distress both to those on the receiving end and for the frustrated manager. (Manzoni & Barsoux, 1998)

The Golem is Jewish myth in which the Golem, a creature of clay said to have been given life by the mystical incantations of the mysterious Maharal, Rabbi Yehuda Loew, leader of the Jewish community of 16th-century Prague. Some versions have Golem as a lovable, clumsy mute; others as a monster like Frankenstein who turned against his creator, giving a vivid warning against magic and the occult. Elie Wiesel in a book entitled the Golem has collected many of the legends associated with this enigmatic and elusive figure and retold them as seen through the eyes of a wizened gravedigger who claims to have witnessed as a child the numerous miracles that legend attributes to the Golem. The Golem is given a shape as the shadow of the Maharal. The Golem was mute and those who did not know him looked down upon him (Wiesel, 1983).

Babad, Inbar, and Rosenthal first conceptualised the Golem effect. They demonstrated it without direct manipulation of the conditions that the subjects experienced in a training situation. The trainees whose instructors expected the least performed worse. Oz and Eden replicated the Golem findings among para-trooper trainees in a true experiment. Ethical considerations inhibit researchers from deliberately inducing low expectations, resulting in researchers focusing on trying to forestall naturally occurring low expectations. Oz and Eden investigated this negative effect using a treatment designed to prevent low expectations from taking root in the minds of instructors toward trainees with relatively low pre-test scores. This design allows investigation of a negative effect that would be unethical to produce experimentally; the effect occurs naturally in the control group, compared to an experimental group subjected to preventive treatment. One study in the Israeli army prevented the natural formation of low expectations toward recruits who had performed poorly in pre-entry fitness tests, by telling some squad leaders that the tests were not indicative of ineptitude. The leaders of the "control" squad were not told how to interpret the test scores of the individuals in their units. At the end of the course, the 'low scorers' in the experimental squads had improved more than those in the control squads, rated their squad leaders more favourably and were more satisfied.

The Golem effect is a deficit in performance that follows the low expectations of the leader. In any environment including work and school, a Golem effect is evidenced by slower growth or poor performance gains among those of whom less is expected (Davidson & Eden, 2000).

The hypothesis tested in a Golem experiment is the same interpersonal expectation-effects hypothesis tested by previous self-fulfilling prophecy experiments conducted in the work environment. That is, when the leader has high expectations, it boosts subordinates' performance,

The negative consequences are substantial. It may cause:

- Lack of employee self-trust and self-confidence
- Lack of trust in peers and superiors
- Disregarded ideas
- Shunning responsibility
- Lower productivity
- Increased chances that employees behave opportunistically
- Lack of encouragement of innovative problem solving

CONCLUSION

The fact that people are able to adjust up or down based on expectations is crucial because, through their behaviour, bosses communicate expectations, as well as influencing the self-expectations of subordinates. The Pygmalion effect is an incredibly powerful phenomenon that can have a profound influence on people's performance and learning. We have seen in this chapter that expectations can have a strong influence on behaviour both positively and negatively. Pygmalion expectations can lead to improved performance, greater motivation, and increased confidence. Gomel expectations, on the other hand, can lead to underperformance and decreased motivation. The Pygmalion effect can also lead to better student outcomes, better teaching methods, and better relationships between teachers and students. The Pygmalion effect is closely related to self-fulfilling prophecy, and the two can work together to create a positive feedback loop that can lead to even better performance. The Gomel effect, on the other hand, delivers the direct opposite. Everyone needs a great level of self-introspection in order to realise your primary source of their own expectation. Are you a beneficiary of Pygmalion or a victim of Gomel? As a writer we have seen in the previous chapter that our great enemy is self-doubt. This chapter has clearly demonstrated through scientific experimentation the source of self-doubt and the source of self-confidence. We hope that this book will be your source of Pygmalion effect and that we will be able to slay the and reduce the power of Gomel on our readers. Remember that you have what it takes to succeed and make the best of your talents. In the next chapter we are going to look into the concept of mindset in detail. We should avoid the characteristics of weaker performers:

- less motivation, less energy; unlikelihood of going "beyond the call of duty";
- more passive; not "taking charge" of problems or projects;
- less proactive; not anticipate problems very well;
- less innovative; tending to "do what they are told" rather than bringing up new ideas;
- more parochial; often lacking in vision and overall perspective;
- more prone to centralise information and authority toward their own subordinates;
- More likely to cause problems; less likely to come up with solutions.

CHAPTER EIGHT

SELF-EFFICACY

In this chapter, we are going to try and explain the reason why you believe that you can do the things that you have been doing and why you are not able to do the thing you believe that you cannot do. We are going to explain this concept using a theory known as self-efficacy developed by Albert Bandura. We would like you to develop a strong faith in your abilities as a writer, that is, strengthen your self-efficacy.

We think it will be helpful to start with the brief history of Albert Bandura and follow his journey towards the development of this theory. In this chapter, I would like you to reflect deeply on your own belief in your abilities and capabilities. Reflect also on your belief that you are not capable of doing certain things or the belief that you may not accomplish certain things. We would like you to be able to point out your earlier influences and even present influences which have shaped your self-believe. In Chapter 1 of this book, we dealt at length about self-doubt and how it develops and takes shape in your life. This book is about equipping you with the tools that will help you succeed.

The late Albert Bandura was born in Canada and passed away in the USA in the town of Stanford and the state of California in 2021 July.

Albert Bandura grew up in a small rural town in Alberta province of Canada. The provinces of Canada rank in size as Quebec, Ontario, and British Columbia. This makes Alberta the fourth largest province. Alberta is bordered in the south by the American state of Montana and in the western side by British Columbia. In the east, it shares a border with Saskatchewan. Finally, in the north by the Northwest Territories (NWT). This province has the rare attribute of being blessed with World Heritage Sites of the United Nations Educational, Scientific and Cultural Organisation. These are the Canadian Rocky Mountain Parks, Dinosaur Provincial Park, Head-Smashed-In Buffalo Jump, Waterton-Glacier International Peace Park, Wood Buffalo National Park and Writing-On-Stone Provincial Park. His parents are of Eastern European descent. His father and mother originated in Poland and Ukraine, respectively. Ukraine is a former Soviet republic. Ukraine is the country that was invaded by Russia in 2021. The war has lasted for more than a year at the time of writing this book. It was not clear how the war would end. Vladimir Putin is reported to have told the Russians that it was not a war, but a special project.

The tensions between Russia and Ukraine are attributed to the desire of Ukrainians to join North Atlantic Treaty Organisation (NATO) as suggested by Volodymyr Zelenskii, the President of Ukraine. The situation began getting out of hand in early 2021 when Putin, the president of Russia, started sending troops near its neighbours Ukraine border. In the beginning, this was dubbed military training exercises in the spring of 202. These exercises increased and continued into the fall. The United States of America, together with its western allies threatened Russia with harsh economic and military sanctions if Ukraine was invaded.

Bandura's parents did not have formal education. His father worked for the company that laid the track for the trans-Canada railroad. He was able to save enough money to purchase a home in those days. In a way, his father was one of the pioneers of the Canadian nation. They constructed Canada and went on to make a great contribution to is country which the Canada today. His school had limited educational resources housed in a single building, where only a couple of teachers taught the entire high school curriculum. After finishing his high school education, one day his mother sat him down to discuss the way forward and find out what he was interested in doing with his life.

The choice was between staying in that area and helping with household chores or going to university. He decided to enroll at the University of British Columbia. He successfully registered at the university. One day, while waiting for class, he went to the library where some student left a course catalogue on the table. While flipping through the catalogue, his eyes were caught by the psychology course. So he unrolled in psychology. This is how he entered the field of psychology, for which he is famous today. He is in the class of great psychologists like Freud. As they say, the rest is history. He argues that this was a choice by fortuity rather than my intention. He and his friend decided to play together when he was still a student. The friend was unable to arrive on time on the golf course. So, they were allocated a later slot in order to accommodate his friend. Before them in the queue were two women, one would later become his wife. These experiences showed him that there is a lot of fortuitousness in our lives (Bandura, 1998). Psychology avoids fortuity and chance like the plague. This does not help the prediction models used in psychology. Bandura started thinking that science should be brought into play on the incidental nature of life.

Coincidence and fortuitousness

The Bandura definition of chance includes the fact that two people who are unfamiliar with each other and have no remote intention of meeting happen to meet. This meeting is not planned. There is no design but fortuity in the chain reaction of the intersection of separate of events in a chance encounter. This despite each even having their own causal determinants,

How many people ended up marring someone they met by pure chance, or moved into their dream occupation or career or even business through the most insignificant situations. An unplanned meeting has a way of determining someone's fate and life path. If you look at your own life, you realise that the better part of your life has been shaped by chance. As someone said, marriage results from proximity, meaning that you can only marry the people you are exposed to. If you were born and grow up in a certain geographic area, you are likely to marry someone from your physical environment. But we find that often people recognise fortuity and acknowledge it only in circumstance when it favours them and refuse to acknowledge it in times of adversity.

The question that we need to answer generally and for ourselves is: Are all our choices the result of our own careful planning and deliberate actions, or do chance-fortuitous, unplanned, and unpredictable events affect the direction our lives take?

Although psychology cannot predict fortuitous events, psychologists should acknowledge that once they occur, they are going to leave you untouched. Fortuitous events can influence people in two possible ways; that is, they can leave you where you are or cause you to branch out into entirely new directions of life. Bandura set up a conceptual scheme to predict the effect of fortuity, depending on peoples own personal attributes and also the nature of the inaugurating environment. He was introducing some sort of novel feature in psychology. He argues that there are two ways in which individuals can exercise some influence given the unplanned characteristic of life. One-way people can influence the probability of chance happening by leading an energetic life style and thus exposing themselves to a lot of different ideas. The second way to make the chance work is by developing one's interests, competencies, and other personal characteristics so that when a fortuitous event occurs, you can take advantage of it.

When he began his research, behaviourism was the dominant field in psychology. According to the theoretical orientation, behaviour is shaped and regulated mainly by rewarding and punishing consequences.

Behaviourism

Other complexities of the modern language could be shaped individually in each member by trial and error. The advent of television meant that televised influences were being pumped into every home. Television networks were working on a false assumption that people crave violence, so most of their programming during the early evenings had a certain amount of violence in them. Families started to be concerned about the effect of violence on their children. The catharsis hypothesis with its assumption that exposure to violence drains aggressive impulses and reduces aggression was dominant at this time. Bandura wanted to know to what extent the aggression was transmitted symbolically. He set up an experiment in which young children observed a model pummelling a doll with a mallet hitting it and then kicking it around the room punching it, throwing it down, and beating it in the face. After the children had observed it on television, he measured the extent to which they picked up exactly the kind of behaviour that was being modelled. What he found was that, in fact, the children are modelling this behaviour and are even activating other forms of aggression not modelled, such as gun play and so on. He began to establish a theory that laid emphasis on the environment as the major source of influence. The Bobo doll created a huge following and made Bandura famous. He was recognised in airports and hotels. In some hotels, such as Washington, the clerk who recognised him as the Bobo doll experimenter gave him a room in the quiet part of the hotel. Another central feature of social cognitive theory is Bandura's ongoing interest in translating individual knowledge into human and enlightenment.

He decided that he can not only promote aggression by modelling, but can also use modelling for therapeutic purposes. Because of this belief, he launched a research programme to develop new forms of therapy based on modelling and guided mastery. He felt that we need to get away from talk therapy and develop therapies in which people confront the problems they have and then enable them to take the steps to change their lives for the better.

He started with the severe snake-phobic who were successfully released from their phobia and in addition, got the corresponding biological changes. The most interesting generalisation made with this finding was the change in the dream activity of these snake-phobic participants. Participants who reported their dreams said things like "I had a dream yesterday in which the boa constrictor had befriended me and helped me wash the dishes. It was really a transformative experience that demonstrated the ability to change. These participants were acting on their own and doing a lot of things that they shared, such as speaking. They had acquired a tremendous sense of efficacy. Bandura decided to shift the direction of his research to focus not just on the modelling part, but he tried to understand how this newly acquired belief system develops and how one builds it.

He developed a theory, and it worked. He was able to demonstrate that it had cognitive influences. He was able to show that whether an individual thinks pessimistically or optimistically affects their level of motivation and the kind of goals they set up for themselves. This also has a bearing on your ability to persist in the face of difficulties. He also demonstrated that this attitude affected their emotional life. This ability to handle stress and depression. The most important finding showed that self-belief or lack thereof affects the decisions people make in critical times. The decisions people make define their life path.

People build self-efficacy through guided mastery through modelling. If they see people who are the same as them struggling and being able to master it, it increases their effort. To see that they can do it, it is built up by people you trust who express faith in your capability in situations where you are going to succeed rather than fail.

These are some of the rewards given to the emeritus Professor Bandura, who was a professor of psychology at Stanford University: the APS William James Fellow Award and the APS James McKeen Cattell Fellow Award. He is a professional psychologist in the world. His research on self-efficacy gained new ground in the study of psychology and proved that beliefs that people hold out their own capabilities affect their choices, determine their level of motivation, and go to an extent of determining the well-being and health of the individual. There is no area of life which has not been touched by self-efficacy. Its has effects even HIV prevention and how teachers teach in their classrooms.

President Obama presented him with the National Medal of Science. This took place 2016 at the White House ceremony in May and recognises over-achievers in the fields of science, technology, and engineering.

President Obama presents Albert Bandura with the National Medal of Science (*Albert Bandura Receives the National Medal of Science*, n.d.).

Self-Efficacy

Now that we have explored the life of the founder of the theory, I think it is appropriate to go into the theory itself. What is self-efficacy?

Like everyone you have a story to tell about your life - where you were born, and what influenced your life. The kind of parents you had and the influence they exerted on you both positive and negative. You also have a story to tell. It can be a happy story, a sad or even one with mixed emotions. No man is an island. As they say we have been raised by the village, the suburb or the township for that matter. Some people even believe that you can take a girl from a shack, but you cannot take the shack out of a girl, or even a boy, for that matter. Which means you may change a person's physical circumstances, such as the house they live in or the car they drive but you cannot change the way the think and behave. Change of behaviour which result from change of thinking is the sole province of the individual. That is why we say you cannot change anybody but yourself. Everybody can change because what we are today is not how we were born but is a result of the influence exerted on us by our environment. But that change can only happen when and if we want it to happen. People in religious organisations like the church are always surprised by the behaviour of people who claim to follow the teachings of Christ. Their behaviour is often contrary to the claims and teachings of the very book to profess to believe in. This is because this people have not made their minds to change but are content to perpetuate the behaviors they learnt from their environments. This is the concept of dissonance.

Dissonance

Dissonance denotes a lack of harmony or consistency between different components. Cognitive dissonance is a theory introduced by psychologist Leon Festinger where he defines cognition as the things a person knows about himself, about his behaviour, and about his surroundings. Dissonance refers to the opposite or counterpart of a fact. The term cognitions also refer to thoughts. Cognitive dissonance is the situation in which two or more cognitions or thoughts are in disagreement with one another. And in practice it may mean that a person says one thing and contradict what they are saying with their actions.

This inconsistency creates a state of psychological tension in a person. Most people often attempt to reduce the dissonance by justifying their behaviour or seeking information that supports their existing beliefs.

Someone told this story with which you may identify with. Her parents were teachers. Her mother was a kindergarten teacher. As a child, her mother took her to work, where she spent much of her time in her mother's classroom. This experience inspired her to become a teacher just like her mother. She eventually became a teacher. After teaching for several years, she wanted to become a coach. She had a greater vision of just being a teacher. Her ultimate goal was to lead teacher professional development training and support teachers with classroom practise. She trusted that she could be good in this role. She applied for a promotion to become a coach; however, her supervisor at the time did not share her vision. The supervisor told her that she would never be a coach. She didn't have what it required to become a coach. She watched in horror as her application gets thrown into the trashcan. She walked out of that office that day devastated. Her self-esteem suffered a serious setback, leading her to believe that maybe her supervisor was right that she does not know how to be a coach.

This shows you how easily our confidence can be broken. It shows how fragile it is. But when she gained her composure after some time, the power of those words was loosening their grip over her day by day. She started to remember that she had a unique ability to connect with learners, which her mother often confirmed to her. She started remembering how her parents fed this great dream she had in mind with words of affirmation. She started believing when she started seeing the difference she was making in the lives of the children she was teaching. She started thinking that maybe her supervisor was wrong and maybe her parents were right. Her resilience started to swell, and she picked up and persevered toward her. She started to believe that she could do it. She knew she could be a successful coach. She applied for a different job and the rest is history.

She now coaches other teacher coaches in her country and even some internationally. There is much that we can learn from this story. Go down memory lane and think of the moments in your own life when you believed in your abilities more than anyone around you ever told you or believed. Belief in our abilities changes how we move towards our aims assignments and encounters. This fundamental faith in our capacity to do well is termed self-efficacy. People with low levels of self-efficacy stop trying if they fail. When they fail at the first attempt, they invent excuses which cause them to give up quickly. At the root of this tendency to easily give up is the lack of faith that they will eventually succeed.

People with higher levels of self-efficacy have been influenced and motivated to try again and again, even in the face of initial failure. They continue to take these actions with perseverance even when faced with challenges. This is a function of self-efficacy; it is a power that drives transformation. It applies to both you and your older self regardless of our profession. What we are looking at in this book is, so how do we get more of this? We also want to help you build self-efficacy. We need to learn to empower ourselves and others to believe in our abilities.

Albert Bandura, the psychologist who developed the theory, classified sources of efficacy beliefs into four categories. The first is to experience success. Success begets success. The more people succeed, the more they believe that they can succeed. The opposite is also true. Coaches and instructors have proven this to be true. When learning any sport, their instructors support them to feel successful as they master each small step towards mastery of their skills independently. The same can be done in teaching people any skill. The task should be broken down into small achievable steps. The instructions can first be individualised.

The strategy should have corresponded to the current skill level. We need to make sure that people feel that immediate sense of success. Positive experience in implementing the skill helps build self-efficacy.

The second source of efficacy occurs when we see others like us succeed. The reason we have low levels of success in poor communities is because children who grow up in these communities do not see people like them succeed. I wrote in my other book The Sanity Gap that I grew up in a township where there were no university educated people. The situation was uninspiring. In most black families in the township and rural area, there are still families with no graduate. Often this is because in that environment children have not seen a graduate in their immediate environment. Here, I giving an example about graduates. But because in this book, we are concerned about developing published authors. You may have the potential to publish, as I believe that everyone can publish. But because you have never met anyone you know personally who is an author, your self-believe may be low as you begin on this journey. Sometimes, you may have to be the pioneer.

Thirdly is Social Persuasion, where encouragement, feedback, and support from others can significantly influence self-efficacy. When you receive positive reinforcement and verbal encouragement from people you trusted, it strengthens your belief in your abilities. The opposite is also true, negative or discouraging feedback lowers your self-efficacy. How many of us affirmed others in our lives on a daily basis? Often we don't even do that for ourselves. Our society treats encouragement and affirmation as if they were a very expensive commodity. We cannot afford not to do it too often. Encouragement is free and is a powerful motivator. We should take advantage of it regularly. We can encourage people with a pat on the shoulder or a positive and kind word. Encouragement always has a positive effect on its recipients. Even when we are not immediately aware of its impact encouragement works!! People will often return and report how our encouraging words and actions have helped them on their life path. People like it when they see their decisions, efforts, and choices being recognised, heard, and appreciated. It helps them to focus more on the progress they are making toward the goal or task that they are currently working on.

The fourth source of efficacy is how we manage negative emotions. Often we mistakenly think that people who are successful never experience negative emotions such as stress and discouragement. We condemn ourselves when we feel down or overwhelmed by the task before us. It needs to be understood that it is natural and normal to feel these negative feelings. However, we should not let our emotions determine what we do next. When emotions take over, our brains become small. Then it becomes difficult to think properly. We needed to find a way to manage our emotions to allow our brain to control the situation.

We have the power to manage our emotions. We do not live in a perfect world. Sometimes even with the best-kept plans things go wrong. We need to plan for that eventuality when things go wrong. We must develop some ways to overcome whatever obstacles we may encounter on the road to reaching our goal. As a writer, you may experience stressful feelings when you have to do new things. When you write, you will learn new tools. You may find it frustrating to learn a new software that you need to edit your work. You will decide how you are going publish your work. You will develop new habits as you unlearn the old unhelpful ones. Let me encourage you and tell you that you can do it, you do not need to panic. Was Rome built in one day? Does a journey of a thousand kilometres not start with the first step? As long-distance runners, we encourage one to say "keep going, you are closer to the finish line than you where you started.

Keep your goals in mind! To reach that goal, you have to do and learn new things. The ideas of Bandura are meant to help you develop greater faith in your abilities and keep going when the going gets tough.

Nothing will delay you like self-doubt. Keep the big picture in mind. Do not allow your big vision to deter you. Break your tasks into small chunks. How do you eat an elephant? - One piece at a time.

F

Figure 1

You may have asked yourself why some people work hard while others do the bare minimum. Bandura's self-efficacy theory helps us to understand why this is the case. Self-efficacy will help us predict whether someone is a high-performer or not. Self-efficacy refers to the level of confidence one possesses in their ability to successfully accomplish a specific goal or carry out a particular task. It involves having faith in one's capabilities and believing that they have the necessary skills and competence to achieve desired outcomes. Self-efficacy is task specific although it has a way of spilling over into other areas of your life. You may have the confidence to manage a mall project and complete it successfully. However, if you are given the same project on a bigger scale, you may feel incompetent.

When someone has recently acquired a new driver's license, they can feel confident driving in their neighbourhood where they learnt to drive before acquiring their license. The same person may feel incompetent driving in the center of town because there is too much traffic. Sometimes they may think that they can drive in the city center but not in a city larger than where they live.

Self-efficacy is not a generalized belief encompassing overall competence or capabilities. Instead, it is a specific belief concerning one's capacity to accomplish a particular task or achieve a specific goal. In the diagram provided, it can be observed that higher levels of self-efficacy correspond to a greater belief in one's ability to successfully perform a task. Conversely, lower self-efficacy leads to reduced confidence in one's capability to carry out a task. The significance of self-efficacy to motivation lies in the fact that individuals are less likely to invest their full effort into a task if they have low self-efficacy regarding that specific task. In other words, if someone does not believe they can successfully complete a task, they are less inclined to exert maximum effort towards it.

Conclusion

The aim of this book is to motivate as many individuals as possible to start writing and become published. We know the obstacles are varied and many. What we have done in this book is to look at the obstacles from a mental or psychological perspective. Our motivation come from the fact we believe that our thoughts inform and direct our behaviour. If we can our thoughts right than to do the right actions become natural. We addressed the still small devastating critical voice. The voice that will accompany us through our journey. We need to drown this voice with the skills we have learnt in book. Otherwise this voice is going to drown. Firstly, to realise that what this voice is telling us is not true. We should not allow this voice to create and exaggerate our self-doubt and unbelief.

We must believe in our own ability to accomplish the task of writing and eventually to get published.

We have also seen that motivation can be affected a a combination of factors. These factors are often influenced by external circumstances, and the specific context of the task or goal. Some of the factors that determine our level of motivation may come down to the fact that people have different personality traits that can influence their motivation levels. Characters such as achievement orientation, self-discipline, and conscientiousness are generally associated with higher motivation. The opposite of the traits as we have discussed in the book at length, like low self-esteem or low self-confidence can hinder motivation.

Goal Orientation: Individuals may have different goal orientations, such as a focus on mastery, performance, or avoiding failure. Those with a strong mastery orientation are more likely to be intrinsically motivated, seeking personal growth and improvement. Performance-oriented individuals may be motivated by external rewards or recognition. Avoidance-oriented individuals may be driven by a fear of failure rather than a desire for success.

Values and Interests: Motivation is often influenced by an individual's values and interests. When people engage in activities aligned with their core values or pursue tasks that align with their interests, they tend to be more motivated. Conversely, if the task or goal is perceived as unimportant or irrelevant to their values, motivation may be lower.

External Rewards and Punishments: External rewards, such as praise, recognition, or tangible incentives, can positively influence motivation, especially in tasks where the external rewards are salient. On the other hand, excessive reliance on external rewards or the presence of punishments can undermine intrinsic motivation and lead to a decrease in overall motivation.

Perceived Competence and Self-Efficacy: Individuals with a higher belief in their own competence and self-efficacy are more likely to be motivated to engage in tasks and persevere in the face of challenges. When people feel capable of achieving success, they are more likely to be motivated to put in the effort required.

Social Context: The social environment can significantly impact motivation. Supportive and encouraging relationships, such as mentors, peers, or a positive work environment, can enhance motivation. Conversely, unsupportive or competitive environments can diminish motivation.

Past Experiences: Previous experiences, especially related to success or failure, can shape future motivation. Positive experiences of achievement can foster a belief in one's abilities and increase motivation. Conversely, repeated failures or negative experiences can dampen motivation and lead to a fear of failure.

It's important to note that motivation is a complex and multifaceted phenomenon, and different individuals may be motivated by different factors or combinations of factors. Additionally, motivation can fluctuate over time and vary across different tasks or goals. Understanding the specific factors that influence an individual's motivation can help tailor strategies to enhance motivation in various contexts.

List of references

Academic Mindfulness Interest Group, M., & Academic Mindfulness Interest Group, M. (2006). Mindfulness-Based Psychotherapies: A Review of Conceptual Foundations, Empirical Evidence and Practical Considerations. *Australian & New Zealand Journal of Psychiatry, 40*(4), 285–294. https://doi.org/10.1080/j.1440-1614.2006.01794.x

Albert Bandura Receives National Medal of Science. (n.d.). Association for Psychological Science - APS. Retrieved 2 February 2023, from https://www.psychologicalscience.org/publications/observer/obsonline/albert-bandura-receives-national-medal-of-science.html

Babbel.com, & GmbH, L. N. (n.d.). *5 African Writers You Should Be Reading*. Babbel Magazine. Retrieved 8 March 2023, from https://www.babbel.com/en/magazine/african-writers

Bandura, A. (1998). Exploration of Fortuitous Determinants of Life Paths. *Psychological Inquiry, 9*(2), 95–99.

Davidson, O. B., & Eden, D. (2000). Remedial self-fulfilling prophecy: Two field experiments to prevent Golem effects among disadvantaged women. *The Journal of Applied Psychology, 85*(3), 386–398. https://doi.org/10.1037/0021-9010.85.3.386

Facing Self-Doubt as a Writer: 7 Tips for Overcoming Writers Self-Doubt. (2022, July 12). https://selfpublishing.com/self-doubt-as-a-writer/

Frontier, C. (2018, September 11). 9 Actors Who Have Struggled with Imposter Syndrome. *Casting Frontier*. https://castingfrontier.com/9-actors-struggled-impostor-syndrome/

Gribble, S. (2021, January 6). 5 Reasons You Should Aim for 100 Literary Rejection Letters in 2021. *The Write Practice*. https://thewritepractice.com/literary-rejection-letters/

Kong, F., Zhao, L., & Tsai, C.-H. (2020). The Relationship Between Entrepreneurial Intention and Action: The Effects of Fear of Failure and Role Model. *Frontiers in Psychology, 11*. https://www.frontiersin.org/articles/10.3389/fpsyg.2020.00229

Mapungubwe—World History Encyclopedia. (n.d.). Retrieved 8 March 2023, from https://www.worldhistory.org/Mapungubwe/

Martina, A. (2018, July 24). 10 Lessons From "Think And Grow Rich" By Napoleon Hill. *Medium*. https://medium.com/@antoniomartina/10-lessons-from-think-and-grow-rich-by-napoleon-hill-3d51e88a7f70

Motive. (n.d.). LII / Legal Information Institute. Retrieved 20 February 2023, from https://www.law.cornell.edu/wex/motive

Open for Discussion: What's the Difference Between Art and Science? (n.d.). American Chemical Society. Retrieved 10 March 2023, from https://www.acs.org/education/resources/highschool/chemmatters/past-issues/2021-2022/april-2022/art-and-science.html

Spitz, H. H. (1999). Beleaguered Pygmalion: A History of the Controversy Over Claims that Teacher Expectancy Raises Intelligence. *Intelligence, 27*(3), 199–234. https://doi.org/10.1016/S0160-2896(99)00026-4

Sutton, A. (2016). Measuring the Effects of Self-Awareness: Construction of the Self-Awareness Outcomes Questionnaire. *Europe's Journal of Psychology, 12*(4), 645–658. https://doi.org/10.5964/ejop.v12i4.1178

The Psychology and Philosophy of Envy | Psychology Today. (n.d.). Retrieved 10 March 2023, from https://www.psychologytoday.com/us/blog/hide-and-seek/201408/the-psychology-and-philosophy-envy

The Pygmalion Effect Explained—Expert Program Management. (2021, March 2). https://expertprogrammanagement.com/2021/03/the-pygmalion-effect-explained/

The Role of the Coach in Elite Athletes' Pre-Performance Routines. (2019, March 29). https://appliedsportpsych.org/blog/2019/03/the-role-of-the-coach-in-elite-athletes-pre-performance-routines/

walterdavis. (2020, January 5). *Pygmalion Factor #1 – Climate*. SlideServe. https://www.slideserve.com/walterdavis/pygmalion-factor-1-climate-powerpoint-ppt-presentation

Wiesel, E. (1983). *The Golem: The story of a legend*. New York: Summit Books. http://archive.org/details/golemstoryof00wies

14 Best-Selling Books Repeatedly Rejected by Publishers. (2007, September 14). HowStuffWorks. https://entertainment.howstuffworks.com/arts/literature/14-best-selling-books-repeatedly-rejected-by-publishers.htm

Andrews, R. (2020, January 23). *How to Combat Self-Doubt as a Writer*. Medium. https://writingcooperative.com/how-to-combat-self-doubt-as-a-writer-1b953f0280f9

Facing Self-Doubt as a Writer: 7 Tips for Overcoming Writers Self-Doubt. (2022, July 12). https://selfpublishing.com/self-doubt-as-a-writer/

How To Overcome Self-Doubt As A Writer · Heart Breathings. (2019, April 25). *Heart Breathings*. https://heartbreathings.com/how-to-overcome-self-doubt-as-a-writer/

Republic, W. (n.d.). *7 Ways to Get over Your Self-Doubt as a Writer | Writers Republic*. Retrieved 15 December 2022, from https://www.writersrepublic.com/blog/get-over-self-doubt-as-writer

Why are writers so prone to self-doubt? - The Writer. (n.d.). Retrieved 15 December 2022, from https://www.writermag.com/writing-inspiration/the-writing-life/self-doubt/

Professor Sello Mokwena is an accomplished academic in the field of Computer Science. He is currently an Associate Professor in the department of Computer Science within the School of Mathematics and Computer Sciences at the University of Limpopo. In this role, he supervises the research of students ranging from Honours degree to PhD level.

Prior to joining the University of Limpopo, Professor Mokwena worked at the Tshwane University of Technology (TUT) as the head of the department. During his time at TUT, he successfully supervised both master's and doctoral students, guiding them to completion. Notably, he made significant efforts to ensure that the research conducted by his students was published in accredited journals, highlighting his commitment to academic excellence.

In recognition of his exceptional research contributions, Professor Mokwena received the institutional award for emerging researcher of the year while at TUT. This accolade further attests to his dedication and scholarly impact within his field.

Beyond his research and supervision roles, Professor Mokwena has also demonstrated his expertise in the area of article publishing. He has conducted a course on article publishing, which has been highly regarded by its attendees for its ease of comprehension and application. This course has assisted numerous individuals in effectively disseminating their research findings.

Additionally, Professor Mokwena is an author and has written a book titled "The Sanity Gap: A Recipe for Not Losing Your Mind." This publication has achieved notable success, with over 1,000 copies sold at the time of writing.

Professor Mokwena's influence extends beyond his own institution. He has actively participated in mentorship programs, collaborating with colleagues from the Universities of Tanzania. Through a mentorship program organized by Deep Learning Indaba Africa, he has contributed to editing and preparing their work for publication in international journals.

Overall, Professor Sello Mokwena is a respected academic, renowned for his research, mentorship, teaching, and expertise in article publishing. His dedication to advancing the field of Computer Science and supporting the scholarly pursuits of students and colleagues is commendable.

He was awarded the best teacher in the School of Mathematics and Computer Sciences at University of Limpopo.

www.ingramcontent.com/pod-product-compliance
Lightning Source LLC
Chambersburg PA
CBHW071359080526
44587CB00017B/3128